Forging Subregional Links in Transportation and Logistics in South Asia

Uma Subramanian
John Arnold

The World Bank
Washington, D.C.

Copyright © 2001 The International Bank for Reconstruction
and Development / THE WORLD BANK
1818 H Street, N.W.
Washington, D.C. 20433, USA

Cover design by Debra Naylor, Naylor Design Inc.

ISBN 0-8213-4885-X

Library of Congress Cataloging-in-Publication Data has been applied for.

Contents

Foreword

"To fight poverty with passion and professionalism for lasting results." This is the very essence of the World Bank's Mission Statement that has a special place in South Asia, a region that harbors a lion's share of the world's poor. Development strategy for poverty alleviation must be rooted in transformation of society by the society. For this, individuals in society must be energized with a vision for their own betterment, and through shared knowledge, resources and capacity building, be helped to translate the vision into reality. Societies that have discovered the magic of individual and collective empowerment are the ones that have discovered the link between political and economic stability and poverty alleviation.

We are rapidly moving to an era of globalization where countries are increasingly connected by markets, trade, finance, resources, transport, information and communication. South Asian countries face a unique opportunity to participate competitively in this global production and trading system. However, this opportunity will be realized only if they can meet the market demands that call for high quality products and services and just-in-time delivery.

This report focuses on a poor sub-region of South Asia covering Bangladesh, Bhutan, Nepal and Eastern India. As the South Asian countries are positioning themselves to participate in global and regional markets in light of recent liberalization policies, their efforts and opportunities to find markets within and outside the region are severely limited due to serious transportation and logistics impediments. These impediments significantly raise the cost of doing business affecting critical economic sectors. In turn, they have an adverse impact on economic growth, low skilled employment and poverty in the sub-region. The landlocked countries or regions are in particular, severely constrained by poor access.

The issues involved in efficient regional transport logistics systems are complex and often politically sensitive. They cut across not only physical infrastructure related bottlenecks, but also policy and procedural issues in the logistics chains—such as red tape and corruption in customs, highly restrictive bilateral protocols on cross-border movement of vehicles, delays and pilferage in ports, and poor modal interfaces. Through the innovative analytic framework that would support more open and rational dialogue among countries and among public and private sector groups in the region, this report would contribute to the process of helping forge partnerships and collaboration in the sub-region, promoting trade, investment, growth and employment.

Let us continue to strive through these and other on-going efforts in the region in our mission to fight poverty.

Mieko Nishimizu
Vice President, South Asia Region
The World Bank

Acknowledgments

The principal authors for this report are Uma Subramanian (task team leader) and John Arnold (consultant). Shunso Tsukada (Transport Specialist) and Peter Yee with S.M Matin (consultants) contributed to the analytic framework and logistics cost data. In addition, Peter Yee, Manmohan Parkash and S.M Matin were responsible for several key background thematic notes that contributed to this report. ALK Associates prepared the logistics cost model, Geographic Information Systems data and maps. Mohammad Iqbal Karim, Surendra Joshi and Harald Hansen provided important inputs as team members. The team is especially grateful to allies and friends from the private and public sectors from the South Asia region who generously shared advice and inputs.

Peer reviewers that include Frannie Leautier, Colin Gannon, Marc Juhel, Anil Bhandari, Thampil Pankaj and T.R. Lakshmanan provided invaluable insights and guidance. We are grateful for guidance from Sadiq Ahmed and input from several colleagues including Eva Molnar, Graham Smith, Ken Gwilliam, Carlos de Castro, Joelle Chassard, Chingboon Lee, Ken Ohashi, Alok Bansal, Stein Lundebye, Guang zhe Chen, Fabio Galli, Mohi Uz Zaman Quazi, Zhi Liu, Uwe Deichmann, Stephan von Klaudy, and Jeffrey Lecksell.

The report was prepared for the South Asia Infrastructure Sector Unit under the management of Vincent Gouarne (Sector Director). Administrative assistance was provided by Gladys Stevens. Halima Samey, Luis Vasquez, Irene Christy, Johana Thapa, and Razia Sultana helped with various aspects in the production and distribution of the report.

Executive Summary

The area of study in the South Asia subregion consists of Bangladesh, Bhutan, Nepal, Eastern India, and the seven Northeastern Indian states. The states included in Eastern India are West Bengal, Uttar Pradesh, Bihar, and Orissa. The Northeastern Indian states include Assam, Mizoram, Nagaland, Arunachal Pradesh, Tripura, Meghalaya, and Manipur. (See Maps 1 to 5 at the end of the report for the key routes considered and the important cross-border points of interest). The subregion, home to half a billion people, is among the poorest regions in the world.

This report synthesizes the work and background reports prepared as part of the sector work under the Bank's South Asia Regional Initiative on Transport Integration. One of the fundamental objectives of this report (in line with the objective of the regional initiative on transport) is to use an analytic framework to identify key transport and logistics impediments that have left the subregion lagging behind in economic growth. A closely linked objective is to improve the access of the landlocked areas in the South Asia subregion, specifically Nepal, Bhutan, and Northeast India, to regional and international markets. The intention is to share the framework and logistics cost model developed with the countries in order to allow stakeholders to continue the process of analysis and dialogue based on updated data as markets, trade, and transport services in the subregion and elsewhere change.

EMERGING TRENDS AND IMPLICATIONS FOR THE SOUTH ASIA SUBREGION

Recent trends in globalization that enable decentralization of production and distribution activities worldwide offer tremendous economic opportunities for employment and growth in poor countries. The ability of countries to grow rapidly depends on their capacity to link with global and regional markets. In turn, this capacity depends significantly on connectivity, and the efficiency and speed with which goods and services can be moved from production centers to final markets. Improvements in transport logistics therefore have important implications for poverty alleviation by offering new economic opportunities

1

through better market linkages, expanded employment possibilities, easier and cheaper development of the resource base, and reduced damages and losses due to inefficient storage and multiple handlings. The rationale for improving transport logistics among countries and with the outside world can also be applied to internal trade between the rural areas and urban markets. Improved transport logistics are very important for small and medium industries in rural areas that must deliver a quality product within an acceptable time and at a competitive cost.

As in other parts of the world, regional and subregional issues are addressed with a great deal of sensitivity in South Asia. Given the sensitivities of regional issues, the Bank study team sought to promote dialogue among key regional stakeholders and provide for a better understanding of key issues and options by learning from experiences in other parts of the world. Its goals were to create a greater popular awareness of the mutual benefits of cooperation and establish a high level of commitment for improved transport logistics, both in the government and the private sector. The Bank team sought to provide technical inputs and a framework to evaluate the broader regional implications of proposals generated by the participants.

The report includes a set of analytic tools that include a geographic information systems (GIS) database for the region and a logistics cost model developed in collaboration with stakeholders in the subregion. The report is not aimed at offering a master plan for a regional transportation network, nor is it envisioned to be a regional transport sector strategy. The broader objective of the report, in line with the objectives of the regional initiative, is to provide an analytic framework and a user-friendly decision support tool to address improved regional movement of goods and services and allow for moving issues from a purely political realm to a more economic and

commercial level (Map 6 at the end of this report). We think that the framework would help lead to improved and rational dialogue in key sectors among and within the countries on substantive issues in the area of transport, logistics, and regional connectivity.

LINKAGES WITH OTHER BANK STRATEGIES[1]

The approach reflects several of the principles under the Bank's Comprehensive Development Framework, including:

- The interactive approach to Advisory and Analytic Activity adopted through continual subnational, national, and regional consultations with stakeholders from various sectors in order to build ownership in the countries.

- Partnership building with and among governments, private sector groups, research institutions, and other development organizations. The task team therefore focused on building allies as well as creating broad coalitions of national stakeholders and development partners from the government, private business groups (such as chambers of commerce, freight forwarders, exporters, and shippers), and donor and development organizations (such as the United Nations and the Asian Development Bank.)[2]

- Knowledge sharing and consultations in order to help develop a joint vision for the subregion that will enable the evolution of national to regional strategies. Toward this

---

1. These other strategies include Country Assistance Strategies and the Comprehensive Development Framework of the World Bank.

2. For more information on the summary proceedings of the Private Sector Consultative Workshop Transport and Trade Facilitation in the subregion, see Background Note 1.

objective, a regional technical workshop was held to offer international experiences on regional integration.[3]

The Regional Initiative on Transport is consistent with country assistance strategies (CAS) for the relevant countries and reflects client interest in the regional dimension for sectoral activities. This was noted in the CAS for India (dated December 19, 1997), the CAS for Nepal (FY98) and Bhutan (FY99), and the forthcoming CAS for Bangladesh. The results of this study can provide information for transport sector strategy updates, such as the Bangladesh and India transport sector updates. It can also provide potentially relevant data for ongoing lending and technical assistance projects, including the Nepal Multimodal Transport and Transit Facilitation project and the Bangladesh Export Diversification project.

METHODOLOGY FOR THE STUDY: SELECTION OF STRATEGIC COMMODITIES AND ROUTES

The core set of strategic commodities and routes selected for this study were chosen for two reasons. First, they provide opportunities for landlocked areas to reach markets and, second, they are critical commodities that link the subregion to the global market. Accordingly, the study examined Bangladeshi exports of garments to Los Angeles and imports of yarn from India; Nepali exports of carpets to Europe and imports of wool from Australia; fruit and processed products from Bhutan to regional markets; and essential consumer commodities to Northeastern India from

the rest of India. The routes included those connecting Nepal and Bhutan to international and regional markets through Calcutta and other India ports, as well as routes linking Northeast India to the rest of India via Bangladesh and on to international markets via Chittagong port.

The analytic framework applied in the evaluation of commodity movements on existing and proposed transit routes took into account both the cost and time associated with the entire logistics chains, including the time and cost for cross-border procedures and moving cargo through seaports (Map 6 at the end of this report). It enabled two types of analysis:

- **Identifying critical impediments along a logistics chain.** Detailed information on physical gaps and constraints, policies, procedures, commodity type, and market conditions helped determine where improvements in the short term can bring about significant returns in terms of efficiency improvements.

- **Comparing alternative routes (and modes) as a means toward the more cost-effective route.** Existing routes were compared with alternative routes that were either already proposed by the private sector or under consideration by the relevant governments, or with those that have some potential for growth. The comparative analysis not only provides information on the potential savings if these routes were operationalized, but it also allows for a dynamic analysis of how improvements in the components of both logistics chains would affect overall benefits and route selection.

HIGHLIGHTS OF THE COMMODITY FLOWS STUDY

None of the routes provided logistics that could be considered fast and reliable, though some of them were more cost effective than others. This

---

3. Specifically, the South Asia Regional Technical Workshop on Transportation and Transit Facilitation, held in April 1999 in Bangkok. It was sponsored by the World Bank and the United Nations' Economic and Social Commission for Asia and the Pacific.

is important as the region moves toward more regional and international trade in higher-value, finished goods. International markets are increasingly demanding tighter and more reliable deliveries. It is clear that improved logistics are essential to remain competitive. Without improvements, the region will not only miss out on new markets, but it will also suffer a decline in market share in existing markets.

The most important constraints in the logistics chains include:

- **Excessive delays in moving cargo through the ports of Calcutta and Chittagong for international trade.** The problems include congestion within the port that leads to inefficient handling of the cargo, cumbersome customs procedures, and delays that stem from waiting for vessels that cannot operate to a fixed day-of-the week schedule because of the uncertainty regarding the turnaround time in the port. This adds to the time for ocean shipment of containers because the movement of the feeder vessels cannot be coordinated with that of the mother vessels, and containers in Singapore have an average waiting time of a week.[4]

- **Inefficiencies at land border crossings.** Significant time delays and logistics costs are due to a combination of impediments. The basic constraints are the lack of efficient customs operations, which cause unnecessary queuing delays for inspection and customs clearance; and a lack of adequate facilities for the transfer of cargo between vehicles and for the storage of cargo that is consolidated at the border. Poor physical planning and lack

---

4. Haldia was not included in the selected routes, although its role in handling the cargoes studied, such as tea, is increasing rapidly.

of coordination in operations cause serious congestion at the busier crossings, such as Petrapole (India)–Benapole (Bangladesh). It also leads to long delays at the less developed crossings where there is no customs office or official in residence, such as at the Banglabandh border crossings in Bangladesh for Nepalese trade cargo.

- **Limitations on routes for transit cargo, regardless of which country the trucks belong to.** This is a significant problem because it prevents the shippers from taking the routes that offer the best balance of time and cost and from selecting the port that offers the least-cost shipping to the overseas destination. This is also true for regional movements.

HIGHLIGHTS OF THE COMPARATIVE ROUTE ANALYSIS

The routes from Nepal, which could use Nhava Sheva rather than Calcutta as a gateway port, would require an initial transfer from road to rail at Moradabad and, later on, at new inland container depots (ICDs) located closer to the origin or destination of the cargo. The longer land transport distance to Nhava Sheva would be more than compensated for by short sailing times to Europe and the potential for direct shipments from Nhava Sheva or transshipment along the route to Europe (instead of backtracking to Singapore, as in the case of Calcutta port).

The shipment of Assam tea on its traditional route through Chittagong is not possible under the current bilateral protocol. Even if there is bilateral agreement on this option, this route offers relatively small savings over the long route around Bangladesh through Siliguri to Calcutta because of the delays at the Akhoura-Agartala border crossing and at the port itself.

The road route between East India and Northeast India through Bangladesh reduces transport distance by more than 60 percent in comparison to the current route around Bangladesh through Siliguri, but it is not open under current protocol. If access for transit cargo to or from Northeastern India were permitted through Bangladesh, the transshipment requirements (the transfer of cargo from Indian to Bangladeshi trucks, and back to Indian trucks) and the cross-border processing delays at the two borders would offset any potential benefits from the reduced distance. However, if border-crossing procedures were significantly reduced and if transit access for Indian vehicles were allowed, there would be significant savings in time and cost.

The rail route between East India and Northeast India through Bangladesh, though also not available under current agreements, may be a feasible one in the medium term as the Indian and Bangladeshi railway systems are increasing compatibility and connectivity.

Among the route-specific observations resulting from the comparative analysis are:

- Seaports are very important factors in determining route selection because of the large delays and high costs for transferring cargo through the ports. The elimination of unnecessary customs procedures and delays in cargo handling will cause cargo to be routed through more efficient seaports.

- Customs clearances lead to unnecessary delays and informal payments. However, they do not have as great an impact as other procedures at border crossings and ports. The uncertainties associated with the delays and costs of clearing customs can often be traced to inadequate preparation of customs documents by the shipper. Customs limitations on working hours, the low supply of officials at the border to clear consignments, the limited number of gates for receiving cargo, and the

lack of transparency of procedures for inspection all reduce efficiency and create animosity. With simplified procedures, standardized documents, and limited inspections, especially for transit cargo, the congestion at the border could be substantially reduced or eliminated.

- The constraints at land border crossings would be significantly reduced if protocols were established for unrestricted movement of cargo across borders in-bond. Instead, there is a provision preventing Indian, Nepalese, or Bhutanese trucks from moving across the Bangladeshi border. India has agreements with Bhutan and Nepal that allow trucks to move across the border, but their movements within the country are restricted. These restrictions add to the cost of transport, not only because of the labor and losses involved in transferring cargo between vehicles, but also because the shipper cannot chose the least-cost provider and the transport companies cannot position themselves to obtain backhaul cargo other than at the border.

- High-value exports from Nepal to the Pacific Rim require faster handling at Calcutta, Chittagong, and Haldia, whereas shipments to Europe and the east coast of the United States require direct (intermodal) connections to the Jawaharlal Nehru Port Trust (JNPT). Both types of shipments require containerization of the cargoes at the earliest point in the logistics chain. The ability to ship in containers will be substantially improved with the operationalization of the three ICDs on the Nepalese border. A direct rail link from Birgunj to the JNPT would provide the greatest efficiency gains among the alternatives considered.

- Truck routes via Bangladesh can offer reductions in time and cost for medium-value goods moving between East India and Northeast India if the cargo can be moved in-bond and there is coordination between customs check-points at border crossings on both sides of Bangladesh to significantly reduce delays and eliminate transshipment. The savings to the shippers should be sufficient to support tolls to cover the cost for road maintenance resulting from the increase in transit traffic.

- For trade in high-value goods between India and Bangladesh, trucks will be the dominant, if not the exclusive, mode. Travel time will be the major concern and route selection will be based on reducing door-to-door delivery time. Significant improvements in rail operations would be needed if this mode were to capture some of this traffic.

- Intraregional shipments of fruits, vegetables, and other perishables from Bhutan and Nepal to India and Bangladesh require much better logistics. This can be achieved by allowing the cargo to move in a single truck from origin to destination and by ensuring that clearance time at the border on both sides does not exceed six hours.

- The extension of the broad-gauge network in India and the development of a dual-gauge network in Bangladesh will offer much broader coverage with much fewer delays. If the Indian and Bangladeshi railways continue to integrate their systems and extend their broad-gauge networks, they might capture some medium-value break-bulk cargoes. However, delays will continue at the border unless compatible rolling stock is introduced and the shortage of locomotives ends. If these capital investments can be combined with more efficient operations, as the Indian organization Concor has achieved, there is the possibility that the railroads can provide the quality of logistics services required by higher-value goods. At a minimum, the railways will be able to maintain market share in their core busi-

ness, the hauling of low-value bulk commodities, because of the higher costs for trucking and the longer transit times for inland water.

- Inland waterways could play a more prominent role in the transport of the low-value bulk cargoes that move between Calcutta and north and east Bangladesh, which is not yet served by broad-gauge rail. The inland water transport network in Bangladesh is of considerable importance for domestic shipments, but it is less relevant for the movement of transit traffic. Very low travel speeds could be compensated for by improvements in channel markings to allow for nighttime navigation and by improvements in port operations to reduce turnaround time. However, this mode is expected to continue to attract only low-value cargoes that can afford long delivery times. An exception is the proposed container-on-barge service between the proposed Patenga port and Dhaka that would take advantage of the poor rail container service and lack of efficient road connections for containers on this major corridor. Another exception would be the countries agreeing to route Numaligarh refinery (Assam) products through Bangladesh to West Bengal.

- Investments in the transport network are necessary to improve the quality of logistics services, but these were given a lower priority than the procedural problems. The lower ranking is due in part to the recognition that these are long-term problems and will require major capital investment and increased private sector participation if they are to be solved. It is also because of expectations that current efforts to improve the transport network in the subregion will yield measurable results over the next five years.

- Trucking is provided almost entirely by the private sector. Truckers use older vehicles with relatively low power-to-weight ratios, suitable for short-haul traffic but not for the long-haul movements of bulk and unitized cargoes. The rates for trucking services are competitive, both within the countries and between the countries, although India has the competitive advantage of not needing to import trucks. The rates are held down by an emphasis on low labor costs and inexpensive equipment rather than by efficient utilization of more expensive, higher-capacity equipment. This is unlikely to change until the road network is improved and regulations regarding truck loads and safety are enforced.

NEED FOR PUBLIC-PRIVATE PARTNERSHIP

The private sector is pursuing improvements in trade relations and transport logistics to ensure a smoother flow of goods and more cost-effective services among the countries in the region. The chambers of commerce of the four countries have established a joint forum called the Emerging East Initiative to examine and promote investment, trade, and the economic growth of the subregion. Participants expressed strong dissatisfaction with the state of freight transportation for regional and international markets and the lack of consultation with users in bilateral and multilateral discussions on cross-country route and mode choices. In their view, the private sector can plan an increased role in the operation and management of landports and logistics services facilities; the development of container transport, container operations, and facilities; cargo-handling facilities and services; and freight-forwarding, customs clearance, financial services, storage, warehousing, general transit, and shipping services at seaports and land border crossings. The private sector delegates' proposals for government action in trade facilitation included:

- Harmonizing government trade and transport policies and regulations in the subregion;

- Amending transit treaties and protocols to allow for a freer choice of transport routes and service providers;

- Instituting a program of modernization for customs and cross-border facilities;

- Increasing the use of container transport by removing institutional impediments, such as the protocol between India and Bangladesh;

- Constructing ICDs in the region to encourage container transport outside the main India rail transport corridors; and

- Improving access to credit and financial intermediation services.

PRELIMINARY AGENDA FOR ACTION

The actions recommended in this report build upon the general theme of consultation with the private and public sectors, and would require action at national and regional levels. Table 1 summarizes short-term and medium- to long-term actions at the national and regional levels. The preliminary agenda focuses on three areas: (a) trade facilitation, (b) coordination of transport sector reform and investment, and (c) development of business-to-business e-commerce. Several actions under the agenda would require action at national levels. Others, such as trade facilitation and improved procedures at the land border crossings, would need a regional mechanism to create regional consistency. At the national level, the recently established national Transport and Trade Facilitation Technical Committees (TTTCs), which comprise key ministries and agencies and private sector representatives, could be the nodal point in Bangladesh, Bhutan, and Nepal. A possible coordination mechanism that has been suggested is a regional technical forum, which would include not only the

TABLE 1   NATIONAL AND REGIONAL ACTIONS: SHORT TERM AND MEDIUM TO LONG TERM

National	Regional
Short Term	
1. Strengthen the Transport and Trade Facilitation Technical Committees (TTTCs) recently established in Bangladesh, Bhutan, and Nepal that are aimed at sustaining interaction between the public agencies and the private sector. These committees now include representation from ministries or departments of commerce, customs, and transport or communication, and private sector representation from chambers of commerce, transport service providers associations, and trade associations. Examine similar institutional options for increased effective dialogue on transport, logistics, and trade facilitation issues in India in the public and private sectors.	1. Establish a regional technical working committee to (a) identify methods for improving logistics for intraregional and extraregional trade, (b) set priorities and short-term targets for achieving the greatest benefits, and (c) develop a forceful and sustainable program for improving logistics in the region. The committee will include: • Government representatives of the relevant trade, transport, and customs agencies to provide the policy and public infrastructure perspective. • Private sector representatives from shippers, consignees, chambers of commerce, and logistics providers to bring a private sector and commercial perspective. • Specialists from other countries and academia representatives to provide best practices knowledge of trade facilitation, supply-chain management, and logistics services, as well as practical limitations on reforms experienced by other regional trade blocs.
2. Technical assistance should be provided to assist transport ministries, development banks, planning ministries, freight forwarders, major shippers, and experts in logistics in the techniques of supply-chain analysis. The logistics cost model developed would provide an easy and adaptable tool for training stakeholders. Procedures should be developed for incorporating supply-chain analysis into decisions regarding investments in transport infrastructure and changes in procedures for cross-border movement. Workshops could be used to inform transport professionals, shippers and consignees, and forwarders of the techniques used in supply-chain management.	2. Regional workshops could be used to share information among transport professionals, shippers and consignees, and forwarders to improve supply-chain logistics in the region. This would be particularly helpful for improving regional and international trade, particularly for landlocked regions.
3. Port reform and modernization for improved performance and logistics is a priority for development of the countries' trade in global markets. The measures would include: • Privatization of port management and operations, • Dedicated private terminal operations to expedite cargo handling, • Facilitating routing cargo through more efficient ports, and • Better coordination of movements between feeder and mainline vessels by improving port performance so the feeder vessels can operate on a fixed schedule.	3. Bilateral (and multilateral) dialogue and agreements can facilitate routing regional cargo through more efficient ports. For instance, routing cargo through more efficient ports on the western coast of the subcontinent could reduce travel time by about one week for exports to Europe.

National	Regional
4. Improve the physical design of land border crossings in high traffic crossings to reduce congestion and delays, with strategic investments in place of the current practice of ad hoc investments. Support private sector involvement in development of superstructure and operations at border crossings.	4. Coordination among relevant countries in effectively improving the physical design of strategic high-traffic land border crossings so that current congestion and delays are reduced dramatically.
5. Simplification of import and export cargo clearance procedures within the countries, including introduction of Automated Systems for Customs Data (or compatible) documentation.	5. Harmonization and standardization of cross-border cargo clearance procedures across countries.
6. Improved communication systems and adoption of automated technology for electronic transfer of information.	6. Compatibility of automated systems for effective electronic interchange of information.
7. Eliminate requirements for transshipment of cargo by trucks at border crossings and move toward increased transit access for vehicles from neighboring countries, so that multiple cargo handling and associated costs and delays are avoided. In addition, introduce: • Automatic weighing of vehicles at border points • Simplified procedures and risk-assessment strategies to replace current cargo inspection practices • Round-the-clock clearance of cargoes at high-density interchange points like Petrapole–Benapole and Gede–Darsana.	7. Revisions of bilateral transit protocols to facilitate uninterrupted movement of transit. Important changes include: • Replacement of the movement of transit cargo in truck convoys to flexible movement against specified time limits with in-bond goods; • The use of secure seals for rail cars or containers carrying transit cargo with very few or no inspections of cargo at the border, other than checking seals; • The Transports Internationaux Routiers (TIR) system for the carriage of goods approved by customs authorities from the transport of sealed containers using the TIR carnet; and • Common vehicle inspection and licensing procedures for trucks used to transport cargo across borders.
8. Monitoring/tracking systmes for cargo movement.	8. More effective mechanisms for monitoring the movement of the cargo, instead of the existing practice of using fixed routes and truck convoys. These could include: • Joint checking of cargoes at the origin and destination; • Electronic data interchange (EDI) between customs facilities within the country and across borders; • Identification numbers, bar codes, or other forms of electronic identification for trucks and cargo containers; • The use of a freight operation information system for real-time monitoring of trains, rail cars, and cargo; and • Tracking systems for transit cargo carried by trucks.

(Table continues on the following page.)

TABLE 1   (continued)

National	Regional
9. Assignment of liability for the carriage of goods within the country to encourage more efficient multimodal transport.	9. Assignment of liability for the carriage of goods and harmonization of this liability scheme across regional and international borders.
10. Development of full rake sidings for rail, night unloading facilities, and terminal facilities at major loading and unloading points.	
11. Development of night navigation facilities on selected inland waterways in Bangladesh and in the waterways linking Northeast India and West Bengal.	
12. For Bangladesh, a cohesive plan identifying key bridges that need upgrading along high-traffic corridors, taking into account ongoing efforts to strengthen bridges on the Dhaka-Chittagong highway.	

Medium and Long term

National	Regional
1. Investments in road network infrastructure, including widening roadways and constructing divided highways. Bangladesh would base this on a review and update of the existing road master plan. India would incorporate planned and ongoing road projects, including the Golden Quadrilateral and West Bengal north-south highway, and a medium-term plan for less congested road links to and among the Northeastern states.	1. Investments at border crossings to facilitate easier two-way flow of traffic.
2. Increased movement of containerized goods, particularly high-value commodities. It would be useful to review (a) the Container Corporation of India (CONCOR) experience and (b) the experience of Nepal ICDs, including efforts to integrate private sector operations and prepare recommendations for making the process more efficient, effective, and transparent.	2. Extend the movement of containerized goods, particularly high-value commodities such as yarn, across national and regional borders.
3. Strengthening and widening bridges where necessary, particularly along selected roadways for Bangladesh and Northeast India.	

National	Regional
4. The TTTCs could oversee a review of the progress and plans for harmonization of rail networks to determine the likely impact on national traffic flows. Other items on the rail agenda would include proposing standards for rolling stock, such as the configuration of container rail cars, the identification system for rail cars, and the introduction of air brakes and semi-automatic couplers for the freight cars crossing the border between India and Bangladesh. Finally the review committee would look at increased private sector involvement in unit train operations, especially proposals for shipping lines and other logistic providers to operate trains for the movement of containers inland.	4. A review of the progress and plans for harmonization of rail networks to determine the likely impact on regional traffic flows. The review should include ways to introduce, expand, and improve block train operations and rail-based ICDs to serve landlocked areas; scope for private sector operations.
5. Modern laws and regulations covering clearer assignment of liabilities for the carriage of cargo, permitting tighter integration of intermodal movements and reducing barriers to entry for potential third-party logistic providers.	5. Harmonization of laws and regulations in the region to enable clear assignment of liabilities for the carriage of cargo and permit tighter integration of intermodal movements across national and international borders. (There is considerable international experience and legal precedence concerning this issue.)

6. Expand e-commerce opportunities more broadly to remote sectors, industries, and regions so that small and medium enterprises can market their products directly to businesses and markets. This would involve:
  • Access to assured data communications and Internet services,
  • Supportive legislation to allow financial transactions over the Internet that are both secure and legally binding,
  • Increased privatization of telecommunications and Internet services,
  • Establishment of a public-private partnership to ensure a competitive environment for e-commerce services, and
  • Training for small- and medium-scale businesses for effective use and development of services.
	6. New systems are needed for improving voice and data transmissions between customs checkpoints at the border crossings and between the checkpoints and central customs offices and seaports. Initially this could be accomplished through a value-added network used by customs. This could be expanded to the ICDs and other border crossings that would act as a center of efficient and effective communications for scheduling and coordinating movements with other activities on the logistics chain. Ultimately, it should allow the users to input data electronically through multiple ports and, eventually, through the Internet.

7. In the long term, systematically introduce measures to move toward offering shippers door-to-door economical just-in-time delivery service, which is important for the country to gain position in the global market.	7. In the long term, systematically introduce measures to move toward offering shippers door-to-door economical just-in-time delivery service, which is important for the region to gain position in the global market.
	8. Implementation of a smart card system for expediting all the transactions associated with cross-border movements.

government and private sectors, but also international expertise.

The analytic framework developed in this report could be used to evaluate other routes as a basic tool for evaluating investments in transport and trade facilitation. The framework should be broadened to consider the impact of delivery time on the perishability of cargoes and the impacts of uncertain delivery times on inventory requirements.

There is need for both short- and long-term improvements. The short-term improvements would address problems related to:

- The exchange of goods between East and Northeast India;

- Bhutanese and Nepali trade with both international and regional markets (in the case of the latter, many commodities have short shelf lives); and

- The trade between Bangladesh and neighboring areas, including Northeast India, and strategic improvements for Bangladesh transport and logistics to improve global trade.

These improvements would also have significant implications for improved logistics in the individual countries. The long-term improvements would focus on the region's capacity to meet the logistics requirements for trade in higher value goods.

The priority problems relating to seaports have to be addressed primarily at a national level. Efforts to reform the port sector in India and Bangladesh are longstanding but have not achieved much, other than private sector initiatives in western Indian ports and the proposed Patenga port in Bangladesh. Port reform is critical for the subregion. Inefficiencies associated with port and ocean transport time can be reduced by routing cargo through more efficient ports and by better coordination between feeder and mainline vessels.

The transport sector reforms, including increased private sector participation in the seaports and railways and the improvements in road capacity and maintenance, are issues that are already under consideration by individual governments. The TTTCs could push for action on these improvements by coordinating private sector advocacy of these reforms and by adding international best practices and benchmarks to the discussion.

Bilateral transit protocols have not provided efficient mechanisms for handling transit cargo, and they instead treat them like import or export cargo. There is a need to end the remaining prohibitions on cross-border movements of cargo, both for regional and international trade. The next step would be to eliminate the remaining requirements for transshipment of cargo between the vehicles at the border. Then it would be necessary to introduce the various procedures used in different trading blocs for the efficient movement of transit cargo.

Simplification of customs documents and procedures and the introduction of electronic data interchange (EDI) systems for direct input by shippers and logistics providers is another important area to reduce constraints at border crossings. Some of the more important reforms that need to be introduced to facilitate cross-border movement of transit traffic as well as bilateral trade are:

- Replacing the movements of transit cargo in truck convoys to flexible movements based on specified time limits.

- The use of secure seals for rail cars or containers carrying transit cargo to eliminate most border inspections, other than checking the seals.

- Common vehicle inspection and licensing procedures for trucks that transport cargo across borders.

- Automatic weighing of vehicles at border points.

- The Transports Internationaux Routiers (TIR) system for the carriage of goods approved by customs authorities from the transport of sealed containers using the TIR carnet.

- Simple procedures and risk-assessment strategies to replace current cargo inspection practices.

- Round-the-clock clearance of cargoes at high-density interchange points like Petrapole–Benapole and Gede–Darsana.

- Development of full rake sidings, night unloading facilities, and terminal facilities at major loading and unloading points.

- Clearer assignments of liabilities to permit tighter integration of intermodal movements and reduce barriers to entry for potential third-party logistic providers. This also encourages railroads and trucking companies to improve quality of service to limit their exposure due to loss or damage of cargo.

In addition, better mechanisms for monitoring the movement of the cargo would include:

- Joint checking of cargoes at the origin and destination;

- EDI between customs facilities within the country and across borders;

- Identification numbers, bar codes, or other forms of electronic identification for trucks and cargo containers;

- The use of freight operation information system for real-time monitoring of trains, rail cars, and cargo; and

- Tracking systems for transit cargo carried by trucks.

The committee should evaluate the alternatives and select those that can be implemented in the next five years. The committee should also look at the longer-term implementation of a smart card system for expediting all the transactions associated with cross-border movements.

BANK GROUP INVOLVEMENT

A fundamental role for the Bank in the regional transport initiative has been that of a convenor, bringing in global knowledge and experience on regional transport and logistics issues, and helping to promote more effective dialogue among the relevant countries and between the public and private sectors.

Four elements of an effective transportation and logistics system for the subregion would be: (a) trade facilitation and logistics improvements, (b) provision of flexible and strategic routes and modal choices, (c) promotion of greater private sector participation, and (d) rationalization of bilateral and regional protocols. For elements (a), (b), and (c), most of the Bank's instruments are critical and add value. Some of these issues are being addressed through ongoing country operations and technical assistance (such as the India National Highways project, the Nepal Multimodal Transport and Trade Facilitation Project, and the Bangladesh Export Diversification project). The strategic impact of country operations, particularly on poverty, could be enhanced if the regional dimension could be more effectively and consistently integrated in country strategies.

Rationalizing regional and bilateral protocol is a historically sensitive issue in South Asia, as in other parts of the world. The Bank's role in this aspect would naturally be small; but this role could be a critical one in providing a more objective and rational basis by bringing in analyses of options and international best practices, and in supporting greater private sector participation. The tools and analysis used in this report could contribute toward this purpose.

In meeting the requirements of the four elements, the opportunity exists for strong partnerships with other development agencies, including the Asian Development Bank, the U.N. Conference on Trade and Development, World Customs Organization, Japanese International Cooperation Agency, and United Nations Economic and Social Commission for Asia and the Pacific. All are involved in regional transport, logistics, and trade facilitation projects in South Asia.

THE REPORT'S AUDIENCE AND ITS STRUCTURE

This report and the complementary outputs are aimed at several audiences:

- People from both governmental agencies and the private sector (such as transport operators and service providers, intermediaries, and other private business officials) in the relevant region, and

- Within the Bank, the individual country work programs for the South Asia subregion and the thematic groups concerned with regional transport.

The first chapter provides an overview of the socioeconomic and economic growth profile of the subregion, the challenges faced by landlocked regions in accessing regional and international markets, and regional and international trade patterns in light of the transport and logistics constraints. It also presents the rationale for the Bank team's role and participatory approach adopted for the sector work. The second chapter examines specific impediments in the transport logistics chain of selected strategic commodity movement in the context of regional and international trade. It focuses on constraints with line-haul movement and impediments at border crossings and at ports. The third chapter provides a framework for a comparative analysis of existing routes with alternative ones, both for the movement of commodities within the region and to international markets. It takes into account all transportation and logistics costs and the availability of physical links. It also addresses issues of modal choice, based on factors such as time sensitivity of the market and the value and perishability of the commodity.

The fourth chapter presents highlights of the constraints faced by private businesses, freight forwarders, exporters and importers, and shippers in the subregion.

The fifth chapter summarizes the key constraints and suggests short-term and long-term options. It also attempts to outline the role that the Bank could play in assisting the subregion to reduce the transportation and logistics constraints.

The sixth and final chapter of the report outlines a preliminary agenda for discussion in the subregion.

1

Connecting a Subregion: A Strategic View

This report synthesizes the work and background reports that were prepared as part of the interactive policy dialogue under the Bank's South Asia Regional Initiative on Transport Integration.[1] It provides a spatial assessment of key transport and logistics issues faced in opening up a region that is lagging in economic growth. The area of study in the South Asia subregion consists of Bangladesh, Bhutan, Nepal, and four Eastern and seven Northeastern Indian states. The Eastern Indian states are West Bengal, Uttar Pradesh, Bihar, and Orissa. The Northeastern Indian states are Assam, Mizoram, Nagaland, Arunachal Pradesh, Tripura, Meghalaya, and Manipur (see Maps 1 and 7 at the back of this report).

The focus of this report is on (a) the costs of doing business within the subregion and with international markets that result from transportation impediments and other logistical issues; (b) an analytic framework to evaluate alternative and cost-effective regional routes; (c) the scope of increased public–private partnerships in the provision, management, and use of transportation services; and (d) identification of priorities for improving regional transportation and logistics services and related policies in the subregion and a discussion on the possible use of World Bank instruments in supporting subregional linkages.

Recent trends in globalization, supported by technological advances in information, communication, and transportation, facilitate increasing decentralization of production, distribution, and supply processes. Outsourcing of component economic activities across multiple countries is becoming more and more common. This process of outsourcing offers economic opportunities to all countries, particularly developing ones, by allowing them to participate in providing value-added services and low-cost raw material or human resource skills. In turn, these countries benefit from improved market access for their exports, acquisition of new technology through international knowledge

---

1. See the list of background notes prepared for this report under the South Asia Regional Initiative on Transport in the bibliography.

transfers, efficiency gains in the economy resulting from increased competitive pressures on domestic economic activities, and increased employment opportunities.

Globalization thus presents economic opportunities. However, the capacity of a country or a region to participate in the global economy and derive concrete benefits is dependent on national and regional policies. Global trade and the associated economic growth of a country or a region depend critically on the efficiency and speed with which goods and services can be delivered from production centers to final markets. Since one-third of world trade in the mid 1990s occurred within global production networks (World Bank 1999),[2] the ability of countries in Mercosur, the Southern African Development Community (SADC), or South Asia to link with these networks and to be more responsive to demand depends on developing an efficient transport and logistics system, which can provide just-in-time and reliable delivery, and ensure quality of cargo. These are important parameters in the emerging global market because market expectations have risen substantially in the last few years.

Within regions or countries, efficient transport and logistics systems offer increased possibilities for linking isolated and landlocked regions to markets and new economic opportunities. The systems also offer easier and cheaper development of the resource base and increased employment opportunities. By facilitating access to a larger regional market, they can help countries benefit from economies of scale. By providing market access to rural areas, they enable rural producers and small industries to deliver quality products within an acceptable time and at a competitive cost. Improved transport logistics systems within the region would encourage growth

_____
2. *World Development Indicators* 1999, The World Bank.

in trade—not only international and intraregional trade, but also domestic trade between rural and urban areas.

The growth of South Asian trade, both with external markets and within the region, is critically dependent on the time and monetary costs of goods movement and cross-border transit of cargo. As the countries are positioning themselves to participate in global markets, the transportation and trade logistics costs must be reduced to at least ensure their current position in the world market. Logistics inefficiencies translate into higher costs of their commodities and, more importantly, have serious implications for the credibility and position of these countries in the international market.

PROFILE OF THE SOUTH ASIA SUBREGION

The subregion, consisting of Bangladesh, Bhutan, and Eastern and Northeastern India, is home to almost a half-billion people. It is among the most densely populated regions in the world. More than half the population lives on less than US$1 a day, and socioeconomic indicators such as infant mortality, life expectancy, and adult and female literacy are among the poorest in the world. Over the next 25 years this population is expected to double, exacerbating problems of poverty, social tension, and environmental degradation, unless strategies for encouraging faster economic growth are conceived and implemented. See Table 1.1 and Table 1.2 for social and economic indicators.

Paradoxically, this region is endowed with abundant natural resources—fertile soil, water, minerals, and energy resources—which are essentially untapped because of poor connectivity and lack of market access. Although the resource potential is large, the interdependencies among the countries are also significant. Both Nepal and Bhutan are landlocked, as are the seven North-

TABLE 1.1   SOCIOECONOMIC INDICATORS

Area	GNP per capita (1998 US $)	Percentage of population living on less than US $1/day	Percentage of population living on less than US $2/day	Infant mortality rate, per 1,000, 1997	Under-5 mortality rate, per 1,000, 1997	Life expectancy at birth, 1997	Adult illiteracy rate, % of people 15 or above, 1997	
							Males	Females
Subregion								
India	430	47	87.5	71	88	63	33	61
Bangladesh	350	50.3	86.7	75	104	58	50	73
Nepal	210	n.a.	n.a.	83	117	57	44	79
Bhutan	430	n.a.	n.a.	63	n.a.	61	n.a.	n.a.
Other Countries								
Indonesia	680	7.7	50.4	47	60	65	9	20
China	750	22.2	57.8	32	39	70	9	25
Argentina	8,970	n.a.	n.a.	22	24	73	3	4
Brazil	4,570	23.6	43.5	34	44	67	16	16
Burkina Faso	n.a.	n.a.	n.a.	99	169	44	n.a.	n.a.
Namibia	n.a.	n.a.	n.a.	65	101	56	n.a.	n.a.
Regions								
East Asia & Pacific	990	n.a.	n.a.	37	47	69	9	22
Latin America & Caribbean	3,940	n.a.	n.a.	32	41	70	12	14
Sub-Saharan Africa	480	n.a.	n.a.	91	147	51	34	50
South Asia	430	n.a.	n.a.	77	100	62	36	63

Note: South Asia includes all the countries in South Asia as categorized in the *World Development Report*.
n.a. = Not available.
Sources: 1999 *World Development Indicators*, World Bank; *World Development Report* 1999/2000, World Bank.

eastern Indian states. In fact, the Northeastern region of India is connected to the rest of the country by a land corridor between Bangladesh and Nepal that is as narrow as 22 kilometers. This landlocked region, a natural hinterland to Chittagong port, trades with the rest of India and the world through this congested land corridor, with high transportation costs. For instance, consider tea exports from Assam that are shipped to Europe via Calcutta port. The transportation cost includes a trucking route of more than 1,400 kilometers through the land corridor around Bangladesh to Calcutta port. The traditional tea route for Assamese tea via Chittagong port would cut the distance down by almost 60 percent. Third-country trade for both Nepal and Bhutan is also routed through Calcutta port, with associated delays and costs.

TABLE 1.2   ECONOMIC GROWTH INDICATORS

Indicators	India	Bangladesh	Nepal	Bhutan
Area (thousand sq. km)	3,288	144	147	47
Population (million)				
1980	687	87	14	n.a.
1998	980	126	23	0.8
Average annual growth rate (percent) 1997–98	2.0	2.1	2.5	n.a.
GNP ($USBillion)				
1998	427.4	44.2	4.9	0.4
Average annual growth rate (percent) 1997–98	6.2	5.9	2.7	8.2
GNP per capita ($US)				
1998	440	350	210	470
Average annual growth rate (percent) 1997–98	4.3	3.2	0.3	6.8
GNP per capita at PPP (percent $US)	2,071	1,330	1,079	1,446
Trade as percentage of GNP				
1970	8.0	17.0	13.0	n.a.
1998	25.0	33.0	58.0	n.a.

PPP = Purchasing power parity.
n.a. = Not available.
Source: *World Development Indicators*, World Bank, 1999.

Historically, South Asian countries have had restrictive trade policy regimes with stringent barriers to cross-border trade, quantitative restrictions and steep tariffs, restrictions on foreign capital investments, and a predominant role of the public sector in the direct production of goods and services and in regulating the private economy. Consequently, the role of trade in the national income of South Asian countries has been historically low. Foreign direct investment flows to the South Asian region have risen in the last decade but remain lower than other regions in the world (Figure 1.1).

Trade among countries in South Asia has been traditionally low during the decades following independence. The rate of growth in exports within the South Asian Association for Regional Cooperation (SAARC) region as a percentage of total exports has been historically low and has stayed low in comparison with other trading blocs such as Mercosur and the SADC (Figure 1.2).

This pattern is reflected within the subregion, with intraregional trade accounting for only a fraction of total third-country trade in each of the countries (Figures 1.3 to 1.6). Trade among the four countries is concentrated in a few key commodities and has not demonstrated much diversification in the last few years. Table 1.3 presents the top 10 commodities traded among Bangladesh, Bhutan, India, and Nepal.

The low official trade figures should also be examined in the context of significant informal trade among the countries concerned. It is estimated that unofficial exports from India to Bangladesh are approximately equal to official exports. The composition of unofficial trade flows is generally complementary to, but markedly different from, official flows. A large portion of the unofficial exports (85 percent) that take place through West Bengal are comprised of food items, live animals (cattle), and consumer goods. The unofficial flow from Bangladesh into India is dominated by a few major products, including synthetic yarn, electronic goods, and spices. A sizeable portion (44 percent) of the unofficial imports consists of gold and Bangladesh currency to pay for Indian goods that are then smuggled into Bangladesh. There is also an unofficial flow of consumer items, such as ready-made garments, from Bangladesh to Tripura. By some estimates this flow is eight to ten times higher than the official flow. The borders between India and Nepal are also porous. According to one estimate, the informal trade between the two countries during the late 1970s and early 1980s could have been eight to ten times higher than the officially recorded trade.

As in other regional trading blocs, such as the ones established by the North America Free Trade Agreement (NAFTA) and Mercosur, regional collaboration in South Asia is complicated by distrust among countries, political agendas that focus on domestic issues, bureaucratic inertia and instability, and infrastructure and logistics constraints. The low levels of mutual trust are reflected in the transport and transit arrangements among the countries in the region.

For example, no foreign vehicle is allowed on Bangladeshi roads. As a result, all products transported by road to Bangladesh from the neighboring countries are transferred onto Bangladeshi trucks at the border, adding to the transportation

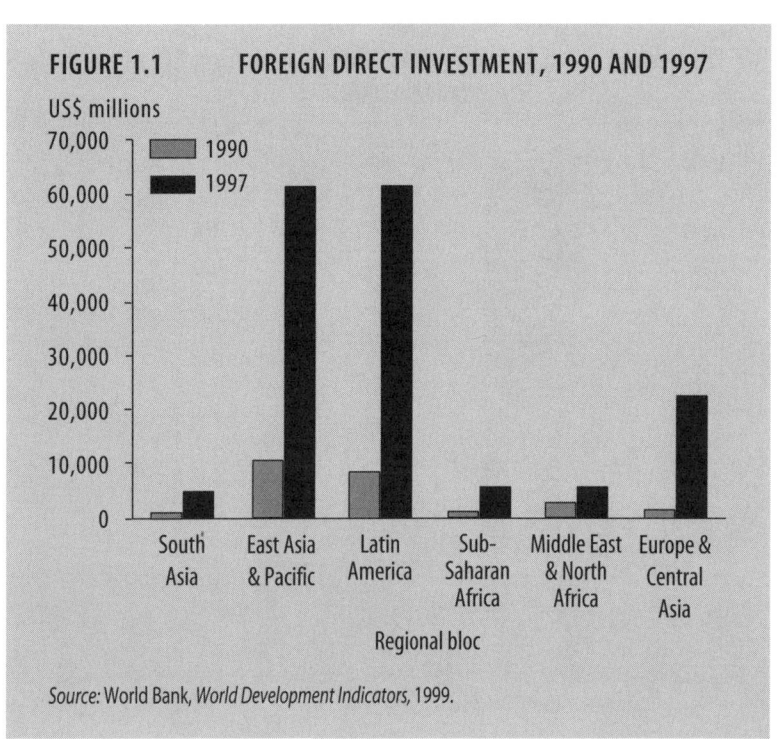

FIGURE 1.1   FOREIGN DIRECT INVESTMENT, 1990 AND 1997

Source: World Bank, *World Development Indicators,* 1999.

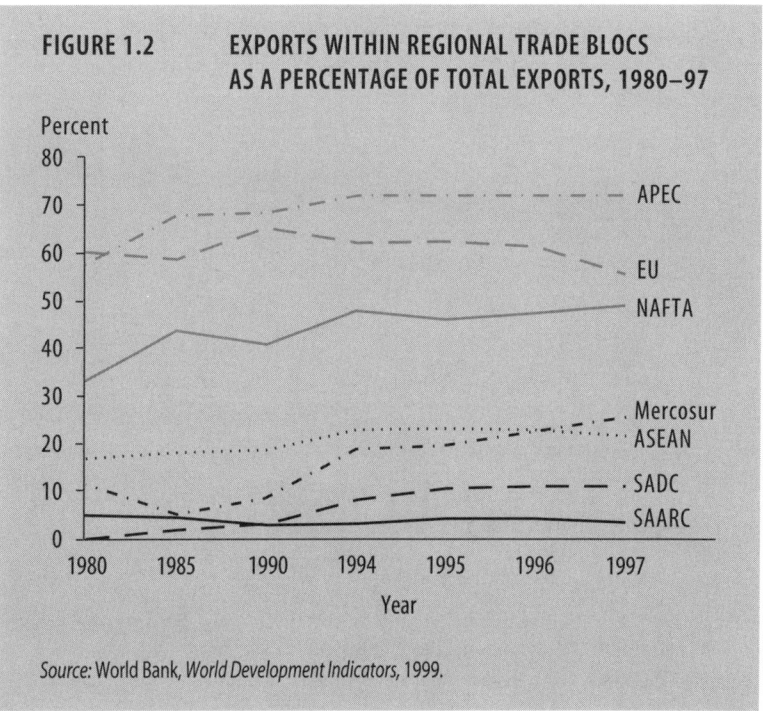

FIGURE 1.2   EXPORTS WITHIN REGIONAL TRADE BLOCS AS A PERCENTAGE OF TOTAL EXPORTS, 1980–97

Source: World Bank, *World Development Indicators,* 1999.

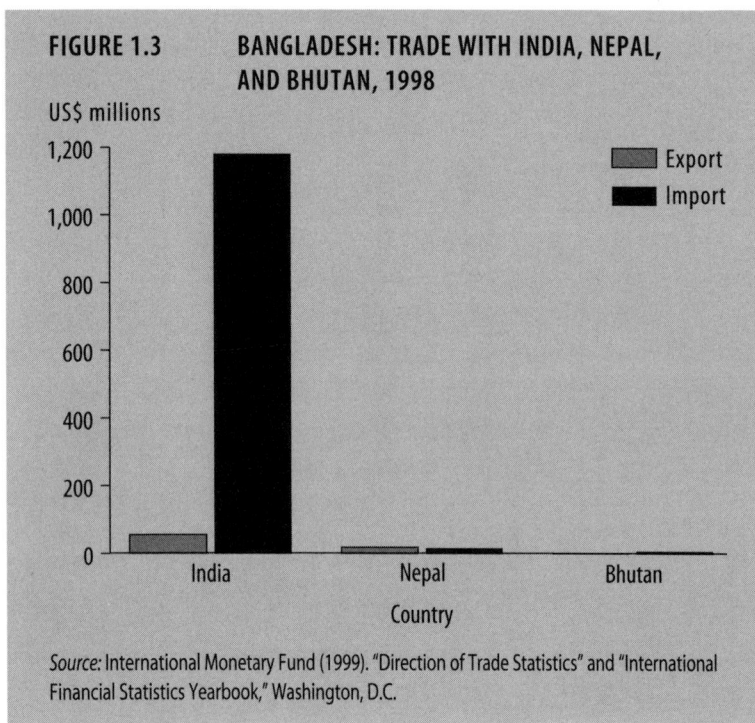

FIGURE 1.3   BANGLADESH: TRADE WITH INDIA, NEPAL, AND BHUTAN, 1998

Source: International Monetary Fund (1999). "Direction of Trade Statistics" and "International Financial Statistics Yearbook," Washington, D.C.

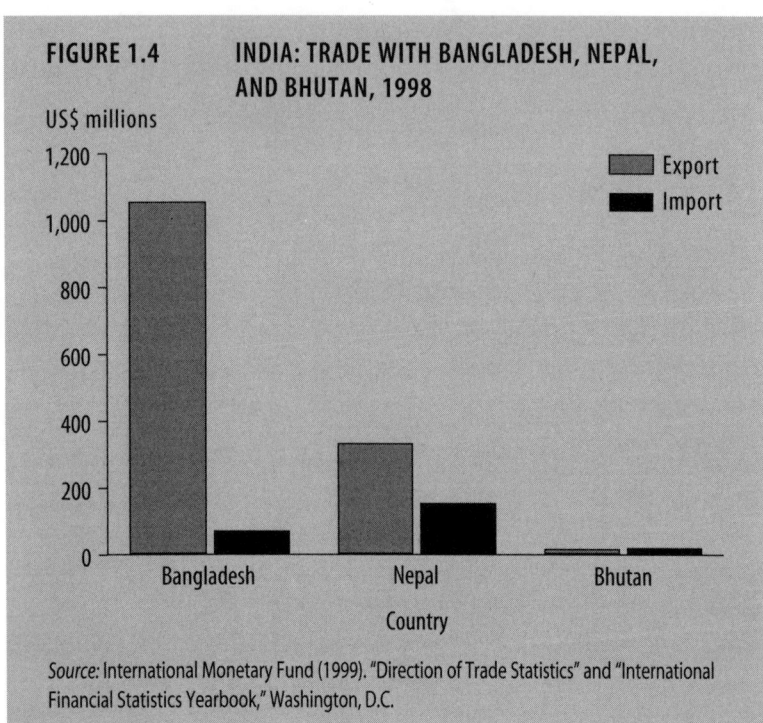

FIGURE 1.4   INDIA: TRADE WITH BANGLADESH, NEPAL, AND BHUTAN, 1998

Source: International Monetary Fund (1999). "Direction of Trade Statistics" and "International Financial Statistics Yearbook," Washington, D.C.

costs and delays at the border crossings. Commodities between the Northeastern Indian states and the rest of India get routed around Bangladesh through India's narrow land corridor (referred to as the "chicken's neck" in the subregion). Nepalese trucks are allowed access only on dedicated routes within India, and Indian trucks that enter Nepal must depart within 72 hours. By one estimate, it takes 45 days to transport a container from Delhi to Dhaka, Bangladesh, because the container moves to Tughlakabad, then to Mumbai, India, and Singapore. From Singapore, the container is shipped to Chittagong port, and then to Dhaka. The distance of 2,000 kilometers between Dhaka and Delhi could be covered in two to three days by rail, according to estimates. But this does not happen because India and Bangladesh lack a proper agreement to move container traffic. These delays illustrate the inefficiencies in the subregional trade system that result from inadequate or nonexistent bilateral and regional agreements.

Inefficiencies at border crossings, which result from a combination of factors, pose another major source of constraints in the subregion. The key border crossing point between Bangladesh and India at Benapole, Bangladesh–Petrapole, India, for instance, through which more than 80 percent of trade gets routed, is severely congested. There are long lines of trucks on both sides of the border (up to 1,500) and waiting times of one to five days. The delays are caused not only by protocol requirements requiring transshipment at the border, but also because of two other important factors: procedural inefficiencies for customs clearances and physical infrastructure constraints (such as poorly designed warehouses and narrow access roads) that do not support efficient utilization of existing capacity.

Ports in the subregion pose a serious constraint to international trade, affecting both national and regional economies. Exporters from South Asia cannot guarantee just-in-time deliveries in the global market. Carpet exports from Kathmandu to Germany, for instance, take almost 50 days to reach a European port. Similarly, the average time to move time-sensitive ready-made garments from Dhaka to Los Angeles is about four to five weeks. In both cases, the delays at the port play a predominant role. Improving port performance would bring direct benefits not only for regional commodity movements but, more importantly, for national economic development. The critical importance of an efficient gateway port for Bangladesh is obvious. The performances of Calcutta and Haldia ports have strong implications for the revitalization of Calcutta and West Bengal.

Perhaps more problematic than the total time is the uncertainty of the actual time of the shipments due to the unreliability of the system. Effective infrastructure links that offer convenient access to markets, supported by rational transport and transit procedures across borders and progressive trade facilitation policies, would offer significant options for this region to develop and enhance intraregional and third country trade.

Impediments to transport and trade facilitation in the South Asian region can be classified as follows:

- Documentation and procedural inefficiencies. The procedures involved in customs inspections, excessive documentation requirements, multiple signatures, lack of transparency, and informal payments lower the efficiency of goods movement and set back regional competitiveness.

- Impediments caused by protocol. These include the various restrictions on cross-border travel of trucks and route choice.

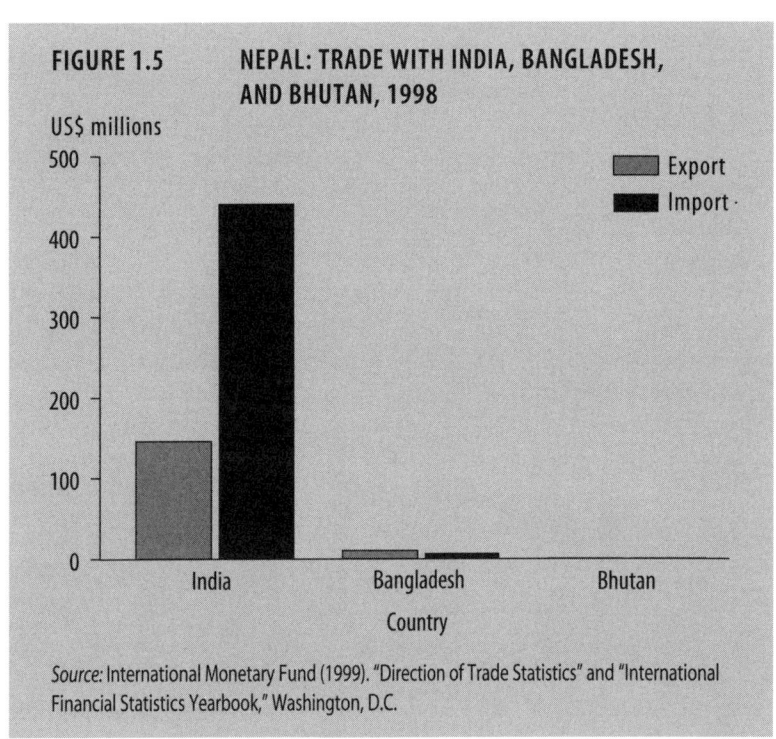

FIGURE 1.5   NEPAL: TRADE WITH INDIA, BANGLADESH, AND BHUTAN, 1998

Source: International Monetary Fund (1999). "Direction of Trade Statistics" and "International Financial Statistics Yearbook," Washington, D.C.

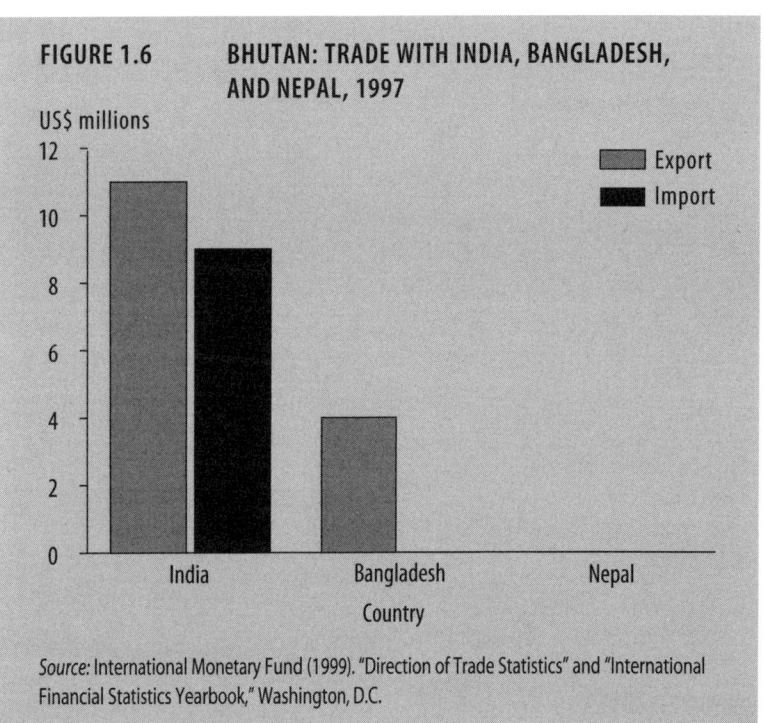

FIGURE 1.6   BHUTAN: TRADE WITH INDIA, BANGLADESH, AND NEPAL, 1997

Source: International Monetary Fund (1999). "Direction of Trade Statistics" and "International Financial Statistics Yearbook," Washington, D.C.

TABLE 1.3 KEY COMMODITIES TRADED IN THE SOUTH ASIA SUBREGION

1996		1997		1998	
Commodities	Percent	Commodities	Percent	Commodities	Percent
India export to Bangladesh					
Total trade	100.0	Total trade	100.0	Total trade	100.0
Textile yarn	31.4	Textile yarn	27.3	Textile yarn	27.3
Cotton fabrics, woven	7.2	Rice	12.3	Rice	12.3
Rice	4.7	Cotton fabrics, woven	7.7	Cotton fabrics, woven	7.7
Motor vehicle parts and accessories	4.6	Lime, cement, building products	4.7	Lime, cement, building products	4.7
Iron, steel, plate, sheet	3.4	Iron, steel, plate, sheet	2.8	Iron, steel, plate, sheet	2.8
Lime, cement, building products	3.3	Coal, lignite, and peat	2.4	Coal, lignite, and peat	2.4
Stone, sand, and gravel	2.7	Motor vehicle parts and accessories	2.1	Motor vehicle parts and accessories	2.1
Cycles, etc. motorized or not	2.5	Rubber tyres, tubes, etc.	2.0	Rubber tyres, tubes, etc	2.0
Rubber tyres, tubes, etc.	2.2	Textile, leather machinery	2.0	Textile, leather machinery	2.0
Aluminium	2.0	Feeding stuff for animals	1.9	Feeding stuff for animals	1.9
Bangladesh Export to India					
Total trade	100.0	Total trade	100.0	Total trade	100.0
Fertilizers, manufactured	92.0	Fertilizers, manufactured	92.7	Inorganic elements, oxides, etc.	44.0
Articles of plastic	7.1	Petroleum products	3.8	Fertilizers, manufactured	38.2
Tea	0.2	Tea	1.2	Tea	5.6
Alcohols, phenols, etc.	0.1	Alcohols, phenols, etc.	0.9	Iron, steel, plate, sheet	2.7
Fish, fresh, chilled, frozen	0.1	Metal tanks, boxes, etc.	0.5	Leather	1.7
Other machinery for special industry	0.1	Leather	0.2	Metal tanks, boxes, etc.	1.6
Under garments not knit	0.1	Textile articles	0.2	Mens outerwear not knit	1.2
Leather	0.1	Articles of plastic	0.1	Under garments not knit	0.8
Metal tanks, boxes, etc.	0.0	Special transactions	0.1	Petroleum products	0.8
Petroleum products	0.0	Floor coverings, etc.	0.1	Womens outerwear nonknit	0.5

Source: UN COMTRADE data, 1998.

- Knowledge and institutional inefficiencies. Because efficient trade facilitation and customs management practices are knowledge- and human capital-intensive, the acquisition of such crucial competency in the workforce is a major challenge for the member countries.

- Physical infrastructure gaps or inefficiencies. These include poor, inadequate, or incompatible physical transportation links; a lack of

such physical facilities as warehouses, parking, and storage at border crossings and ports; and a lack of terminal facilities.

RECENT DEVELOPMENTS IN THE SUBREGION

Since the late 1980s, and especially since the early 1990s, there has been a clear shift from the protective trade regime. Most South Asian countries have adopted policy reforms that have made their economies more open to the rest of the world, and they have promoted greater interest in intraregional trade. India, Pakistan, Bangladesh, Sri Lanka, Maldives, Nepal, and Bhutan established SAARC in 1985. The agreement began with the SAARC Preferential Trading Arrangement (SAPTA). The countries now are pursuing initiatives to establish the South Asia Free Trade Area (SAFTA).[3]

At both the regional and subregional levels, there has been further interest in the last decade in improving links among the countries. Relations have begun to thaw both because of the political leadership of the respective countries and because of SAARC and the planned creation of SAFTA in the near future.

As in other parts of the world, this drive toward regional cooperation in South Asia is occurring in the context of major changes in the economic institutions in these countries—growing liberalization, deregulation and decontrol of industries and markets, reduction in the economic role of the state, and an expanding role for the private sector. Although these processes are still nascent, there has been a steady increase in the share of trade to GDP, and a growing economic dynamism that is reflected by the robust income growth in the last decade, which is second only to that of East Asia (World Bank 2000).[4] The share of trade to GDP is 25 percent. Figures 1.7 to 1.9 show the improvement in export performance consequent to trade reforms, with Bangladesh's export growth particularly impressive. The share of manufactured exports as a proportion of total goods exports also shows rapid growth.

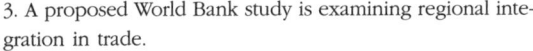

3. A proposed World Bank study is examining regional integration in trade.

4. *World Development Report* 2000, the World Bank.

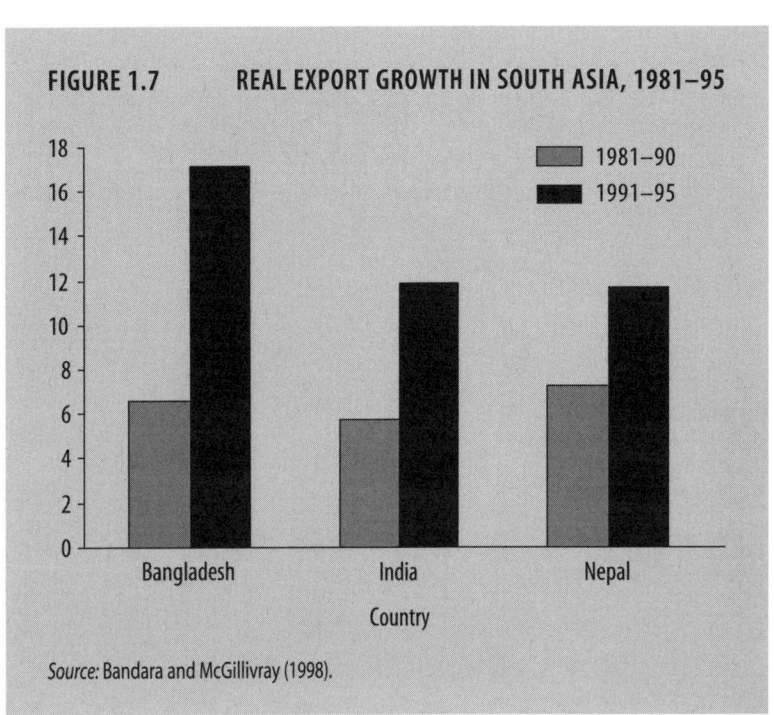

FIGURE 1.7   REAL EXPORT GROWTH IN SOUTH ASIA, 1981–95

Source: Bandara and McGillivray (1998).

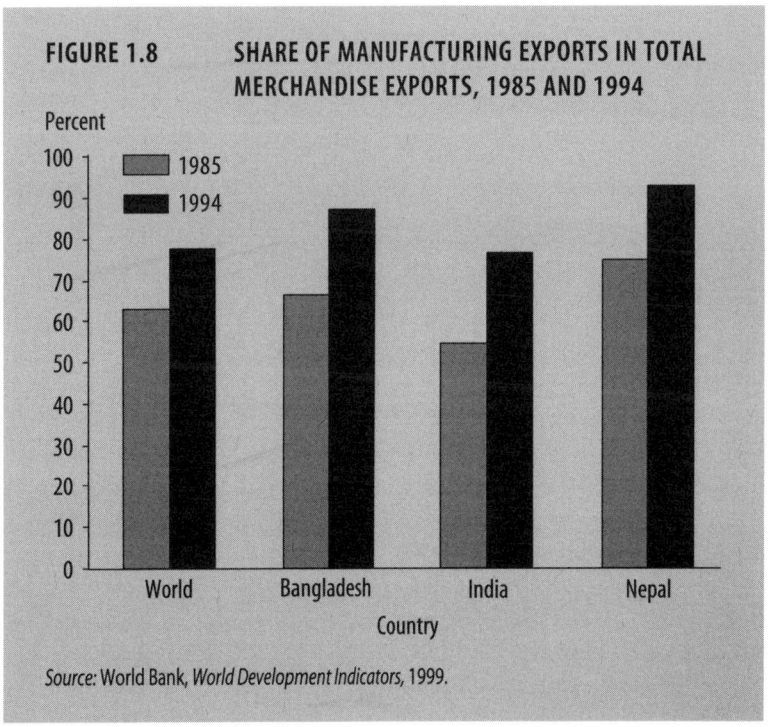

FIGURE 1.8   SHARE OF MANUFACTURING EXPORTS IN TOTAL MERCHANDISE EXPORTS, 1985 AND 1994

Source: World Bank, *World Development Indicators,* 1999.

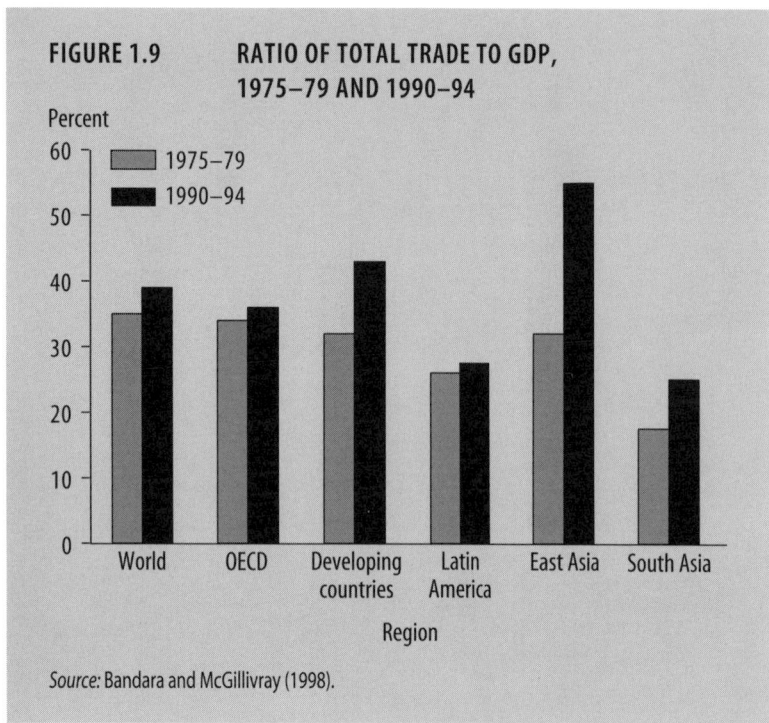

FIGURE 1.9   RATIO OF TOTAL TRADE TO GDP, 1975–79 AND 1990–94

Source: Bandara and McGillivray (1998).

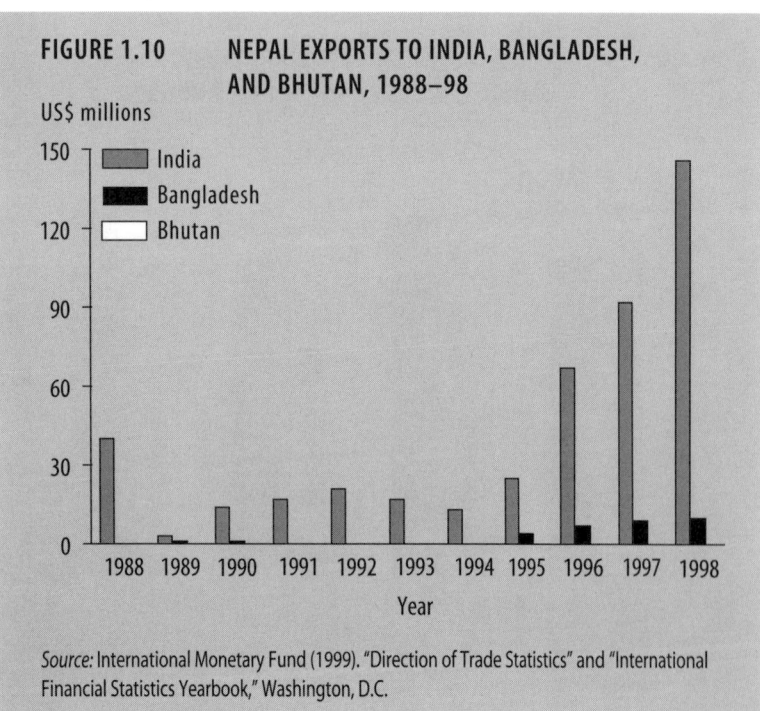

FIGURE 1.10   NEPAL EXPORTS TO INDIA, BANGLADESH, AND BHUTAN, 1988–98

Source: International Monetary Fund (1999). "Direction of Trade Statistics" and "International Financial Statistics Yearbook," Washington, D.C.

Though intraregional trade is only a fraction of total trade, and the growth rate of intraregional trade as percentage of total trade has been slow, in terms of absolute value there has been a multifold increase in intraregional trade in the last decade (Figures 1.10 to 1.12). Between 1988 and 1998, India's exports to Bangladesh increased in value terms by over six times, while exports from Bangladesh to India increased four to five times. A similar pattern has emerged for Nepal–India trade. Trade between Bangladesh and Nepal and Bangladesh and Bhutan has also begun to rise, though not so steeply.

With economic liberalization, there is slowly mounting domestic and international private sector interest in the region. The Indo–U.S. Joint Council Summit in December 1997 in Calcutta brought prominent private sector groups from the United States and South Asia to examine opportunities for investment.[5] On January 15, 1998, the prime ministers of Bangladesh, Pakistan, and India, accompanied by business delegations from each of the countries, met at a business summit in Dhaka to discuss issues related to the establishment of regional energy grids, as well as improvements in trade relations and transport logistics to ensure a smoother flow of goods and services among the countries. Local business communities are pursuing improvements in trade and transport logistics to improve the flow of goods and services and enhance communications among the countries in the subcontinent.

In the area of transport and trade facilitation in particular, there have been several important developments in the last two or three years that clearly indicate the beginnings of change. The following need to be supported:

5. The World Bank was represented by the India country management team member.

- The Emerging East Initiative is a key private sector development within the subregion to promote economic growth, development through improved investments, trade, and transportation in the subregion. In 1998, the chambers of commerce of Bangladesh, Bhutan, India, and Nepal signed a joint memorandum of understanding to this effect.

- A "subregional quadrangle" consisting of Bangladesh, Bhutan, India, and Nepal was formed in 1998 under the auspices of SAARC to examine development opportunities in several sectors.

- India and Bangladesh renewed the Inland Waterways Transit Treaty in October 1999. They removed some of the anomalies that have existed for the last few decades, allowing for a more equitable transit opportunity that should benefit both countries.[6]

- Bangladesh and India launched a direct bus service between Dhaka and Calcutta in March 1999.

- Transshipment for Indian cargo through Bangladesh is being debated in Bangladesh. If well conceived and regulated, this effort could benefit the eastern and northeastern parts of India and Bangladesh. This debate has been ongoing since fall 1999.[7]

- India and Bangladesh are engaged in sustained efforts to integrate their railway systems. Both railways have completed the work for open-

6. The Numaligarh refinery in Assam is already examining options to move refinery products via Bangladesh inland waterway route to Calcutta.

7. The Bangladeshi government has commissioned a study to examine transshipment options under the Bank's Export Diversification Project.

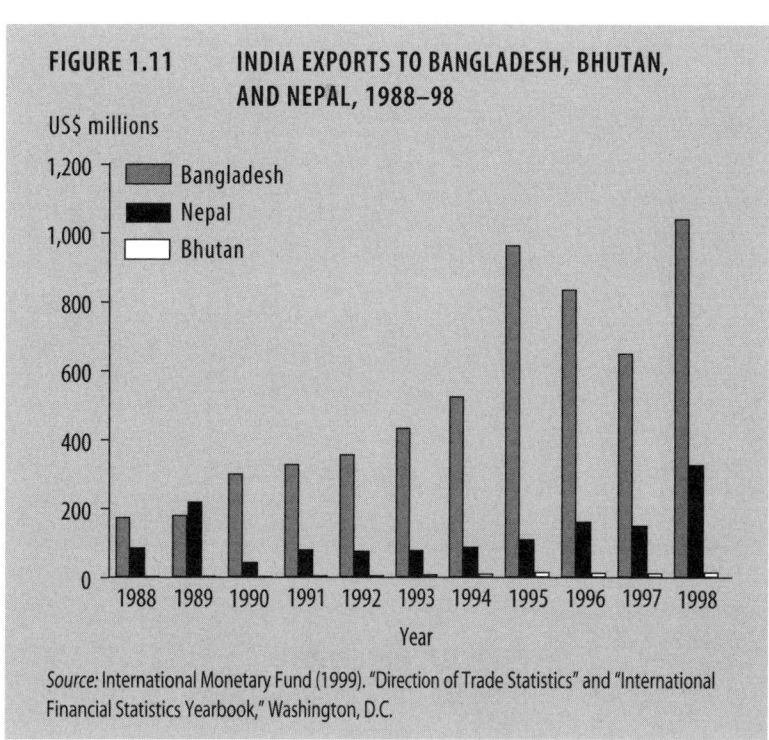

FIGURE 1.11   INDIA EXPORTS TO BANGLADESH, BHUTAN, AND NEPAL, 1988–98

Source: International Monetary Fund (1999). "Direction of Trade Statistics" and "International Financial Statistics Yearbook," Washington, D.C.

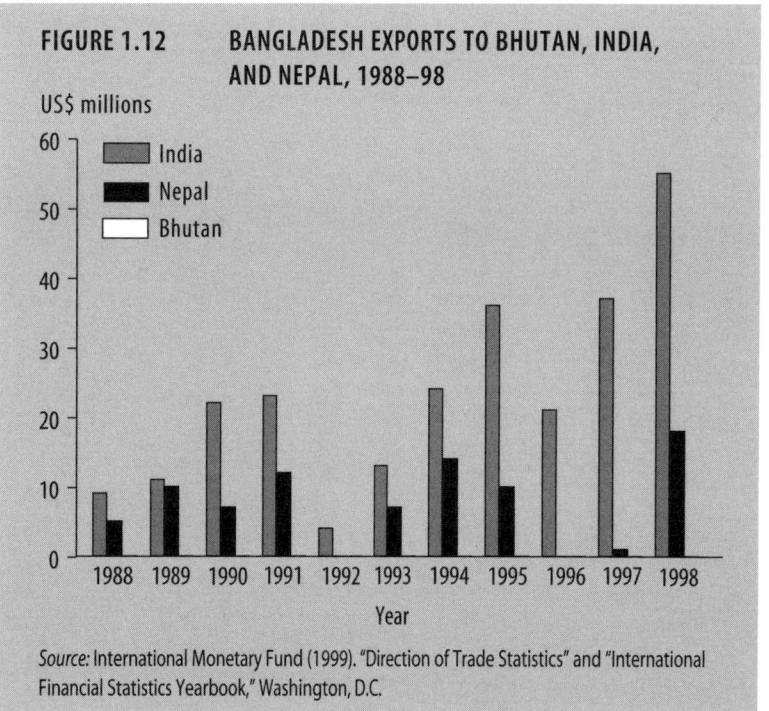

FIGURE 1.12   BANGLADESH EXPORTS TO BHUTAN, INDIA, AND NEPAL, 1988–98

Source: International Monetary Fund (1999). "Direction of Trade Statistics" and "International Financial Statistics Yearbook," Washington, D.C.

ing the entry through the Petrapole–Benapole border crossing, in addition to the three existing crossings on the western side of Bangladesh. On the eastern side of Bangladesh, plans to connect rail links between Akhoura, Bangladesh, and Agartala, India, have already been agreed to by the two countries.

- The governments of Bangladesh, Nepal, and India signed the Phulbari treaty in 1998 to allow Nepalese goods access to Bangladeshi markets.

- Bangladesh introduced preshipment inspection on a mandatory basis in the spring of 2000.

POTENTIAL FOR GROWTH: THE NEED FOR A SHARED VISION

As illustrated by such developments as the establishment of the subregional quadrangle, the stakeholders in the subregion clearly see that development would be effectively realized by:

- A long term vision in which the economies are more closely integrated, and are characterized by global and intraregional transport, trade, and investment activities;

- New economic opportunities that provide employment, attract domestic and foreign investment, and provide the essential basis for more rapid economic growth;

- Optimal development and management of the rich natural resources of the region; and

- Private sector-led growth in an enabling policy environment.

The realization of these goals is related to the ability of the countries to grow rapidly. In turn, this ability is dependent upon the countries being well linked to global and regional markets, and upon the efficiency and speed with which the countries are able to move goods and services from production centers to final markets. Improvement of transportation networks and logistics not only facilitates these links to global and regional markets, but it also increases the potential for cross-border integration of manufacturing and service activities and the potential for exploiting the economies of scale in a larger regional market. These changes would have significant implications for opening up one of the poorest regions in the world.

An example of expanding to regional markets is that of Bhutanese fruit and fruit products finding markets in Bangladesh and India. Nepal is also trying to expand its market for agricultural products (such as jhumla apples) to Bangladesh and India.[8] The Northeastern Indian states have good potential to find markets in Bangladesh for horticultural products that are currently confined to local markets or informally traded across borders for low prices. Similarly, the Northeastern states could obtain fish from Bangladesh instead of having it transported from Andhra Pradesh, Bihar, West Bengal, and Uttar Pradesh. It is estimated that the Northeastern states get 90,000 tons of fish per year from these other states.[9] According to the report of the Committee on Clause Seven of the Assam Accord (1990), Assam was spending almost as much to transport essential commodities such as grains, fish, and edible oils from "mainland" India as for the commodities

---

8. The Phulbari treaty that allows Nepalese cargo access to Bangladesh via a new route through Banglabandh was supposed to facilitate this trade. Though there are physical and logistical constraints that impede free flows, Nepal is keen to extend the treaty.

9. The estimate comes from B.G. Verghese's 1996 book, *India's Northeast Resurgent: Ethnicity, Insurgency, Governance, and Development*, published by the Centre for Policy Studies, New Delhi, India.

themselves.[10] The Indian-Bangladeshi trade groups, as well as policy research groups in the countries, have identified a number of possibilities for collaborative ventures in such areas as fertilizer, cement, and gas-based industries.[11] For both Nepal and Bangladesh, ready-made garments are the top export commodity for international markets.

In discussing regional transport and logistics systems, a fundamental question that is often asked is: To what extent does the economy of the transit country benefit from improvements in transport and logistics systems? The country providing the transport infrastructure could, in principle, recover its investment through appropriate charges to the transit vehicles and cargo while deriving added value from complementary services provided to these transport activities. The value added is greatest when the transit country provides an efficient international seaport gateway and some of the trucking or rail services used in the logistics chain.

A more critical question that is of direct relevance to our work in South Asia is: To what extent do transport logistics improvements benefit the poorer members of society? The more immediate benefits would be better access to domestic and foreign markets for local products and increased employment associated with upgrading the transport infrastructure. The medium- and long-term benefits are the continuity and even expansion of employment in economic activities or industries that, without better logistics, would either not have been established or would have

rapidly lost market share. The extent and allocation of benefits would, of course, be affected by:

- How well the isolated or landlocked regions are served;

- The extent to which the new economic activities are labor-intensive;

- How the charges are structured (who pays and who benefits); and

- How efficient are the logistics systems that will help minimize cost to the economy.

The experiences of countries in other regional trade blocs such as Mercosur, NAFTA, and SADC could provide insights to South Asia, because the region is looking increasingly toward both global markets and greater trade and investment relationships within the region.[12] An example for South Asia is that of Rotterdam port, which has maintained its position as one of the world's largest ports for four decades. There are clear lessons in Rotterdam's experience for managers of ports and airports in developing countries as they organize their trade and transport chains. Rotterdam has retained its prominent position in the global transportation networks by:

- Acquiring the knowledge and competency necessary to offer its customers and industrial tenants state-of-the-art trade and transport chain services; and

- Engaging in strategic scanning of the larger economic and transportation environment, identifying adaptive future paths in the context of emerging change trends, and keeping up to date by implementing the relevant physical, human, and institutional investments.

---

10. Ibid.

11. The possibilities were discussed at the 1995 meeting, Indo-Bangladesh Dialogue: Economic and Trade Cooperation. The Center for Policy Dialogue, India, and the Center for Policy Dialogue, Bangladesh, hosted the meeting as part of an ongoing dialogue between nongovernmental and research groups.

12. For a more detailed discussion of global case studies on regional integration, please see publication, *Integration of Transport and Trade Facilitation*, 2001, World Bank.

APPROACH

As this chapter mentioned earlier, the countries in the subregion are only slowly beginning to open up to each other and to external markets. As in other parts of the world, regional and subregional issues are still addressed with sensitivity. Given the political sensitivities of regional issues, the study team did not adopt the standard models in sector work or project preparation for the work under the Regional Initiative on Transport. Instead the approach adopted under the Regional Initiative on Transport sought to build confidence among key regional stakeholders, support increased dialogue, provide for a better understanding of key issues and options by learning from experiences in other parts of the world (such as NAFTA, the European Union, Mercosur, and the SADC), create a greater popular awareness of the mutual benefits of cooperation, and establish a high level of commitment in both the government and private sectors.

The approach reflects several of the principles of the Bank's Comprehensive Development Framework:

- The interactive approach to advisory and analytic activity adopted through continual subnational, national, and regional consultations with stakeholders from various sectors in order to build ownership in the countries.

- Knowledge sharing and consultations in order to help develop a joint vision for the subregion that will enable moving out of national strategies to regional strategies. To move toward this objective, a regional technical workshop on transport and transit facilitation was held in Bangkok in April 1999.[13] Regional

stakeholders from the government and private sector were able to draw lessons for South Asia from international experts on global regional integration cases. The proceedings and the recommendations that emerged from intensive discussions among the delegates at the regional workshop were discussed in national consultative meetings in the countries to determine priorities for the countries.[14]

- Partnership building with and among governments, private sector organizations, research institutions, and other development organizations. The task team therefore focused on building allies as well as broad coalitions of national stakeholders and development partners from the government, private business groups (such as chambers of commerce, freight forwarders, exports, and shippers), donor and development organizations (such as United Nations agencies and the Asian Development Bank). Private sector representatives of the four relevant countries were invited to participate in a consultative workshop at a regional meeting in Kathmandu to discuss the principal constraints they face in their operations and examine options for improving transport links and trade in the subregion.[15]

- An integrated and cross-sectoral approach that takes a comprehensive view while identifying specific short- and medium-term solutions for a region that could well be one of the world's poorest pockets.

---

13. The April 1999 Bangkok workshop was called the South Asia Regional Technical Workshop on Transportation and Transit Facilitation. The World Bank and the United Nations Economic and Social Commission for Asia and the Pacific sponsored it.

14. Proceedings of the Regional Technical Workshop on Transportation and Transit Facilitation can be found on the World Bank website at: http://www.worldbank.org/html/fpd/transport/publicat/twu-34.pdf. The presentations are available in pdf format at: http://www.worldbank.org/html/fpd/transport/tr_facil/present.htm.

15. Please see Background Note 1 for a summary of discussions at the regional private sector meeting in Kathmandu.

In its country operations, the Bank and the countries themselves are confronting development issues that have regional implications. The Regional Initiative on Transport is consistent with CAS for the relevant countries and reflects client interest in the regional dimension for sectoral activities as noted in the CAS for India (dated December 19, 1997), Nepal (1998 fiscal year), and Bhutan (1999 fiscal year) and the forthcoming CAS for Bangladesh. There is significant synergy with the transport sector strategies, such as the Bangladesh Transport Sector update and the forthcoming India Transport Sector update, as well as with relevant ongoing lending and technical assistance projects (such as the Nepal Multimodal Transport and Transit Facilitation project and the Bangladesh Export Diversification project). The work has strong synergy with the transport and trade facilitation work performed by other development agencies, including the Asian Development Bank, United Nations Conference on Trade and Development, and United Nations Economic and Social Commission for Asia and the Pacific.

This report contains a set of analytic tools that include a Geographic Information Systems database for the region and a logistics cost model developed by the Bank study team in collaboration with stakeholders in the subregion (Map 7 at the end of this report).[16] Together they provide a strategic framework for identifying key impediments ranging from physical infrastructure gaps, gaps and inefficiencies in services at transshipment points and border crossings, constraints at border crossings and ports, an analysis of alternative routes for moving strategic

commodities for regional and international trade, and, more importantly, a transparent and user-friendly analytic instrument that will allow improved and more information-based dialogue among countries and between the public and private sectors on regional and bilateral trade, transit, and transport protocol.

Consistent with the overall approach of the regional initiative, this report does not purport to offer a master plan for a regional transportation network, nor is it envisioned to be a regional transport sector strategy. The broader objective of the report, in line with the objectives of the Regional Initiative, is to provide a strategic framework for improved and rational dialogue among the countries, as well as among key sectors in the countries, on substantive issues in transport, logistics, and regional connectivity. Instead of single solutions, it offers an analytic framework and a user-friendly decision support system to address improved regional movement of goods and services, allowing for moving issues from a purely political realm to a more economic and commercial level. As the countries are privatizing and reaching out to global markets, it is becoming more apparent that intrinsic dependencies and comparative advantages must be exploited so that the subregion can open itself to new economic activities. The analysis starts with the premise that strengthening the linkages among the countries is not a zero-sum game.

This report and the complementary outputs are aimed at several audiences:

- People in both government agencies and private sector organizations (including transport operators and service providers, intermediaries, and private business officials) in the relevant countries and regions.

- Within the Bank, the report complements the individual country work program. At the network and thematic groups level, the work and

---

16. In addition, a report that compiles international case studies of transport and trade facilitation arrangements in selected regional trading blocs is also available. Please see publication, Lakshmanan, T. R., U. Subramanian, B. P. Anderson, F. A. Leautier (eds.). *Integration of Transport and Trade Facilitation: Selected Regional Case Studies*. The World Bank, 2001.

the analytic approach and tools developed add to the knowledge management base, contributing to the regional transport work being done in other regions of the Bank.

For the analytic framework we took a microeconomic, practical hands-on approach that evolved with close work with the private sector in the subregion. The analytic approach helped us not only determine distance and transportation costs, but also time, reliability, and cargo safety, including market and commodity characteristics.

In order to understand how well the markets and transportation of commodities work, we chose strategic routes and commodities. Because our larger objective was to open up a subregion that had been lagging, the selection of the strategic routes and commodities took into account the regional development aspect as well. From the sample route and commodities studies, we get an in-depth understanding of impediments in transportation and other logistics in moving commodities on existing routes to regional and international markets.

We then looked at promising route linkages to understand what makes some routes more cost-effective than others, whether they could be further improved, and why the more cost-effective routes were not being used. The results of the analysis allow us to point to specific problems regarding specific commodities and routes, as well as to more general problems affecting the subregion:

- Border crossings that include ports are a critical cause of delays and logistics costs.

- There is a need for greater flexibility in transporting cargo between routes and between modes of transportation, not only because of the characteristics of markets and commodities, but also because of fundamental changes occurring in international trade and logistics.

The report does not attempt to define specific investment projects, nor does it attempt to quantify the larger benefits to the economy from improved regional transport and logistics. The analysis provides insights into cost savings to the private sector for specific routes and commodities through transport and logistics efficiency improvements and different route choices. The savings from improved transport logistics systems can produce significant cost savings to the private exporter, importer, and shipper. However, as a percentage of the costs of delivered goods in the final market, the logistics costs in the studies in this report—although higher than international standards—are not outrageously higher. The reason, of course, is that transport logistics costs are a small part of the overall delivered costs of goods, except for very low-value goods (such as cement and limestone). The important point to note here is the underlying and more dynamic implications of poor logistics and higher associated transport costs. The real benefit of improved transport logistics are reduced delivery times, more reliable deliveries, and increased cargo security, all of which are critical parameters in the emerging global market in which market expectations have risen substantially in the last few years.

Though the countries in the region (to varying extents) have started to liberalize trade, make their industrial sectors more efficient, reduce government involvement in commercial activities, and improve transportation networks and institutions, they have not been as assiduous in improving the logistics systems to the same extent. Failure to address logistics inefficiencies not only compromises the extent and depth of other reforms, but it also threatens loss in market share and could weaken the current competitive edge of these countries in providing low-wage work forces. Examining the garment sector alone, the implications include (a) fold: loss of employment to a large unskilled and semiskilled workforce, and (b) denial of the same workforce opportunities to upgrade skills and income as the market dictates higher-grade products.

STRUCTURE OF THE REPORT

This first chapter has provided an overview of the socioeconomic and growth profile of the subregion. It examined regional and international trade patterns in light of the transport and logistics constraints. The second chapter examines specific impediments in the transport logistics chain of commodity movement in the context of regional and international trade, focusing on constraints with line-haul movement and on impediments at border crossings and ports. The analysis draws heavily on origin-to-destination studies of selected strategic commodities for each of the concerned countries.

The third chapter provides a framework to examine alternative routes for the movement of commodities, either within the region or to international markets. It takes into account all costs of transportation and logistics and the availability of physical links. Issues of modal choice based on factors such as time sensitivity of market, commodity value, and commodity perishability, are also addressed. Although the chapter presents the key constraints and opportunities in the subregion in terms of strategic linkages and areas for priority attention, it does not advocate one physical route over another. We believe that international routings are best determined by the concerned stakeholders that include governments, network users, and service providers.

What we have attempted to do is provide a rational framework under which such decisions can be made in a participatory transparent manner, in which those who will be affected can move beyond purely political considerations to commercial and economic considerations.

The fourth chapter highlights the constraints faced by private businesses, freight forwarders, exporters and importers, and shippers in the subregion. The constraints and options that we present reflect the views of the private sector participants from the subregion at the regional consultative meeting hosted by the Bank in February 1999 in Kathmandu, which we mentioned earlier.[17] In addition, the chapter also presents some innovative private sector initiatives in the subregion in the area of transport.

The fifth chapter of the report summarizes the key constraints in transportation and logistics. It discusses the broad set of options for consideration in the countries. It also attempts to outline the role that the Bank could play in assisting the subregion reduce its transportation and logistics constraints.

The sixth and final chapter outlines the next steps that would be important to consider for national and regional action in the short and long terms.

---

17. Summary proceedings of the Consultative Workshop Transport and Trade Facilitation in the subregion. Please see Background Note 1.

2

Reducing Logistics Costs

Efforts to facilitate trade among India, Nepal, Bhutan, and Bangladesh, and between these countries and the rest of the world, must look beyond improvements in the transport network to a general strengthening of entire logistics chains.[1] These chains include the complete set of services needed to move cargo from its point of production to points of sale or consumption. An effective trade regime requires a full range of efficient logistics services with tight integration between them. Each link of a logistics chain must have sufficient capacity and a simple and effective interface with the preceding and following links. The type of logistics services required for cross-border trade varies depending on the goods that are being transported and the markets for these goods. High-value, time-sensitive goods require more sophisticated logistics so that they can be delivered to the market in good condition as quickly as possible. Low-value, time-insensitive goods require simple logistics that reduce the overall cost of transport and provide reliable consistent service. In both cases, the objective is to reduce transaction costs as much as possible—which involves a balancing of the cost, time, safety, and reliability of delivery.

The following analysis of the shipments within the region divides logistics into the following three basic services:

- Line-haul transport. This may be by road, rail, inland water and ocean, and it may include intermodal transfers.[2]

---

1. Over the last 50 years, the scope of analysis of transport services has been expanding. In the 1950s and 1960s, engineering analysis was used to examine specific components of a transport system, such as a port, a road link, or an airport, or such subcomponents as a berth, intersection or runway. In the 1970s, systems analysis was used to evaluate the interaction between the links and modes of transport networks. The emergence of multimodal transport in the 1980's extended this analysis to multimodal routes and intermodal interchanges. Toward the end of the century, the growing emphasis on door-to-door movements and just-in-time shipments shifted attention to logistics and to market analysis.

2. Air transport was not included in this analysis although it is of increasing importance in the movement of high-value goods.

No.	Route links	Mode on land	Commodity
Domestic			
1	Calcutta-Gauhati-Agartala	Indian rail	Cement
2	Calcutta-Siliguri-Agartala	Indian truck	General freight
Regional			
3	Calcutta-Narayanganj-Ashuganj-Agartala	Indian-Bangladeshi barge/truck	Cement
4	Kathmandu-Phulbari-Dhaka	Nepalese-Bangladeshi truck	Agricultural produce
5	Thimpu-Burimari-Dhaka	Bhutanese -Bangladeshi truck	Limestone
6	Calcutta-Benapole-Dhaka	Indian-Bangladeshi truck	Yarn
Third country			
7	New Zealand-Calcutta-Rauxal-Kathmandu	Indian-Nepalese truck	Wool
8	Karimganj-Calcutta-United Kingdom	Indian truck	Tea
9	Kathmandu-Rauxal-Calcutta-Germany	Nepalese-Indian truck	Carpet
10	Singapore-Calcutta-Jaigaon-Thimphu	Indian truck	Polypropylene
11	Dhaka-Chittagong-United States	Bangladeshi truck	Cotton garment

TABLE 2.1   CHARACTERISTICS OF SELECTED ROUTES

Source: Logistics cost study data, World Bank.

- Border crossings. These are at seaports and land borders.

- Complementary services. These include both physical services, such as storage, consolidation and repackaging, and commercial services, such as trade finance and insurance, customs clearance, transfer of shipping documents, and interbusiness communications.

The analysis is supported by a detailed examination of the logistics components for the commodity-route combinations listed in Table 2.1. The routes were selected because they include strategic commodities, emphasize cross-border movements, and serve landlocked countries and isolated areas such as Northeast India. Using the logistics cost model developed by the Bank team in close consultation with private sector groups in the region, the study team conducted intensive interviews with freight forwarders, clearing and forwarding agents, shippers, and truckers to obtain data on charges for logistics services, time to complete different activities, and specific impediments on each of the routes for selected commodities.

The routes are divided into domestic routes that are restricted to a single country, regional routes that involve cross-border movements among the four countries, and third-country routes that involve ocean shipping to countries outside the region. The first group has an advantage because it does not face any cross-border delays.[3] The second group has problems associated with cross-

3. We have not included constraints in crossing state or province borders within countries.

border movements and transshipment between the vehicles of two countries. The third group has the additional problem of moving cargo through the seaports. Maps 1–5 at the end of this report present some of the routes and the border crossing points.

TRANSPORT COMPONENTS

Line-Haul Transport

Because most of these routes involve cross-border movements, and half involve shipments to countries outside the region, it is essential to look at the modal interface. This requires an understanding of the capacity and performance of individual modes within a country and their compatibility with bordering countries. India and Bangladesh have all four modes of transport, whereas Bhutan and Nepal have only road transport.

Road Transport

The primary mode for freight movements is road transport. Medium-size trucks (seven to ten ton payload) operate over two lane asphalt roads (5.5 meters wide in Bangladesh, 5.5 to 7 meters in India) at relatively low average speeds. Table 2.2 shows the characteristics of road transport. Only small portions of the major corridors are dual carriageways, and few of these are outside the large cities. Only recently has India begun to upgrade its four major intercity roads to dual carriage ways (Box 2.1). Many of the major roads are poorly maintained and congested. The result is relatively low average travel speeds, in the range of 200 to 400 kilometers per day. The movement of containers[4] on the Indian roadways

is limited not only by the design and condition of the roads and traffic congestion but also by nonphysical barriers to moving containers out of the port. Tractor-trailers are also rare because of their cost, as well as road conditions, congestion, and weight limits. In Bangladesh, the weight limits on the bridges between Chittagong and Dhaka, the main corridor for containerizable goods, prevent the use of tractor-trailers.

Most of the trucks used in cross-border movements are two- to three-axle (six- or ten-wheel) trucks carrying payloads up to 18 tons. Trucks carrying bulk cargoes are generally overloaded,

---

4. These containers adhere to standards set by the International Organization for Standardization, which is based in Switzerland.

TABLE 2.2   CHARACTERISTICS OF LINE-HAUL TRANSPORT

National roads	India	Bangladesh	Nepal
Max. axle load (ton)	10	8.2	n.a.
Typical truck GVW (ton)	15	11	12
Typical truck payload	10	7	9

Railroad Rail gauge	E India Broad	NE India (BG/MG)[a]	Bangladesh (BG/MG)[a]
Typical engine (BHP)	2,600	2,600/1,350	2,000–2,300/ 1,350–1,650
Max. axle load (ton)	20.3	20.3/ 12.7	22.5/13.0*
Car payload (ton)	58.8	58.8	40.0
Typical train length (feet)	2,200	2,200	1,800
Typical train length (car)	40 bogie	40/35 bogie	35 bogie
Avg. travel speed (kph)	23.7	23.7/18.1	11.0/12.3
Max. travel speed (kph)	100	100/65	80/72
Train control	Block telecom	Block telecom	Tokenless block

a. Broad gauge/meter gauge.
* Limit due to Jamuna Bridge 18.0.
n.a. = Not available.
Source: Consultant estimates.

BOX 2.1   INDIA'S "GOLDEN QUADRILATERAL" ROAD NETWORK

The National Highways Authority of India has given priority to the development of a divided highway connecting the major cities of Mumbai, Delhi, Calcutta, and Chennai. The Golden Quadrilateral has a total length of almost 6,000 kilometers, of which about one-fifth is either completed or under construction, and another two-fifths is in the planning stage. Most of the project will consist of widening the existing two-lane roads. A recently negotiated World Bank loan will support the construction of the link between Delhi and Calcutta.

In addition to the quadrilateral, the authority is planning 7,300 kilometers of north-south and east-west dual carriage highways. About one-tenth is either completed or under contract. This project is scheduled for completion in 2009.

The estimated cost of Rs.54 billion for these projects will be financed through a variety of mechanisms, including fuel taxes, external borrowing, and tolls. About 10 percent will be funded through private concessions.

When completed, these roads are expected to reduce the travel times between the major cities and to allow for a dramatic increase in movement of containers by road. This assumes that the port regulations limiting full container loads movements are eliminated. These roads will greatly improve the access of Nepal, Northeast India, and Bhutan to the major ports of India.

causing additional damage to the road. Those carrying containers, garments, or other high-cube (low-density) cargoes have payloads of 10 tons or less.

The load limit for Indian roads is 10 tons per axle. Bhutan and Nepal have similar limits. Bangladesh currently applies a limit of 8.2 tons per axle, but this is expected to increase to 10 tons. The size of vehicles is limited by the capacity of the bridges, many of which are old, narrow, and in need of strengthening. The limits on total gross vehicle weight vary among the countries, but are below the level required for efficient operation of larger trucks and tractor-trailers. The combination of weight limits and road conditions make it expensive to move bulk commodities long distances by road unless the trucks are overloaded.

For-hire trucking services in all four countries are provided almost entirely by the private sector. Most of the trucking companies are relatively small, with fewer than 10 trucks. Strong competition produces relatively low freight rates. These rates and the lack of strict inspection standards discourage the use of new trucks. As a result, the average age of the fleet in Bangladesh is 15 years. The fleets in India and Nepal are slightly younger, with long-distance trucks less than five years old, on average. Most of the trucks are manufactured in India or Japan and have relatively low power-to-weight ratios. The combination of the age and condition of the vehicles, market conditions, slow travel speeds, and short travel distances creates relatively low average truck utilization—about 50 thousand loaded kilometers per year.

As Table 2.3 shows, the cost of road transport per kilometer is relatively low because of a combination of low labor costs and less expensive vehicles (in terms of capital rather than maintenance). However the lack of backhaul cargoes and the small payloads of the trucks increase operating costs. The capital costs for Indian trucking are significantly lower than for neighboring countries because the trucks are locally produced. However, as Table 2.3 indicates, the neighbor-

TABLE 2.3   ESTIMATED TRUCK OPERATING COSTS

Country	Per km	Per ton-km [a]
India – 15 ton	$.0.33	$0.044
India –12 ton	$0.33	$0.049
Bangladesh –11 ton	$0.27	$0.048
Nepal – 10 ton	$0.31	$0.046

a. Assuming 50 percent backhaul.
Source: Background Note 2.

ing countries are able to compete on routes within their own countries.

Despite the differences in road dimensions and national limits on gross vehicle weight, there are no physical hindrances on the movement of trucks between the countries. Any constraints on cross-border movements are caused by insufficient capacity on the roads approaching the border, inadequate waiting area and customs checkpoints, and the lack of effective transit protocols. For example, Bangladesh does not allow trucks from other countries to travel on its roads. India reciprocates but does allow trucks from Nepal and Bhutan to operate on designated transit routes. Indian trucks are allowed into Nepal and are given a limit of 72 hours to carry cargo and return to India. Additional data on truck transport is provided in Background Note 2.

Rail Transport

The rail networks in India and Bangladesh are a mix of broad (1.68 meters) and meter gauge (Table 2.2). In India about one-third of the system is double tracked, whereas in Bangladesh the percentage is much smaller. India has made a concerted effort to convert its network to broad gauge and Bangladesh has undertaken some conversions to dual gauge. The network in Eastern India is mainly broad gauge. However, the connecting links with Nepal are meter-gauge rail with the exception of Birgunj (which is a broad-gauge link). The rail link between Radhikapur and Birol is also a meter-gauge line. The network in Northeast India is meter-gauge, except for a broad-gauge line extending to Lumding. The next section to Kumarghat is currently being converted to broad gauge. The section extending from Kumarghat to Agartala is being constructed as a broad-gauge alignment.

The network in eastern Bangladesh is meter gauge whereas the western part of the country has predominantly broad gauge. The construction of the rail link across the Jamuna Bridge and the extension of dual-gauge operations to Dhaka are expected to be completed next year, substantially improving the coverage of the broad-gauge system. Several other harmonizations are either underway or being planned which will provide additional linkages between the western and eastern parts of the country.[5] In addition, the planned introduction of dual-gauge track between Chittagong, Akhaura, and Tongi will provide a direct link between Chittagong and both Nepal and northeast India. Although the strength of the track and type of sleepers differs between the two countries, this does not prevent the movement of rail cars across the border.

The Indian and Bangladesh railways are publicly operated. Despite recent efforts to improve performance, they continue to suffer from overstaffing, poor maintenance, and old rolling stock. Bangladesh Railways also suffers from poor utilization of equipment (Table 2.4A and B). In Bangladesh there is also a significant problem with track maintenance, especially in areas prone to flooding. Although rail is the second most important mode of transport in both countries, it has suffered a declining market share due to operational problems. Rail traffic has been declining in both relative and absolute terms. In Bangladesh, the tonnage declined by about 40 percent over 25 years while market share decreased to 7 percent of total tonnage. The market share is continuing to decline but the traffic tonnage has flattened out. Rail share in India,

5. Two other projects under consideration are the linking of Akhaura and Agartala, which the Indian and Bangladesh Railways are undertaking, and a proposal to link Tongi and Akhaura utilizing German funds. A link between Dhaka and Joydepur is expected to be completed next year with dual-gauge connections between Joydepur and Parbatipur.

TABLE 2.4A RAILWAY PERFORMANCE INDICES, 1969–70 TO 1997–98				
	Bangladesh railways		Indian railways	
	BG[a]	MG[b]	BG[a]	MG[b]
Car kms/day	20.9	16.6	169.1	38.2
Engine kms/day	149	170	396	331
Bangladesh	1969–70	1996–97	1997–98	1998–99
Route kms	2,858	2,706	2,733	2,733
No. of locomotives	486	284	275	279
Freight cars in FWUs	19,616	15,917	15,073	14,247
Tons carried (in millions)	4.88	2.94	3.04	3.42
Ton-kms (in millions)	1,265	782	804	896
India	1970–71	1996–97	1997–98	1997–98
Route kms	59,790	62,725	62,495	62,809
No. of locomotives	11,158	6,975	7,206	7,429
Freight cars in FWUs	383,990	272,144	263,981	253,186
Tons carried (in millions)	167.9	409.0	429.4	420.3
Ton-kms (in millions)	235,785	277,567	284,249	281,513

a. Broad gauge
b. Meter gauge
Source: Bangladesh Integrated Transport Sector Study, 1998; see also Background Note 3.

TABLE 2.4B MODAL SHARE OF TRAFFIC IN BANGLADESH			
Bangladesh (modal share)	1974/75	1984/85	1996/97
Road	35	48	63
Rail	28	17	7
Water	37	35	30

the operations. The principal rail cargoes are bulk cargoes, both liquid and dry.

In India, the movement of containers by railroad has increased substantially following the formation of Container Corporation of India and the procurement of a large fleet of cars for transporting standardized boxes. In Bangladesh, the transport of containers is limited by the lack of cars and the operating commitment of the railroad. There are some block train movements between Chittagong and the Dhaka ICD, but these account for a very small portion of the containers handled at Chittagong (Background Notes 3 and 4). Problems with rail services, charges, and port regulations limit the amount of boxes that are moved between the port of Chittagong and the Dhaka ICD to about 15 percent of the total volume moved through Chittagong. At least 40 percent of containers going from Dhaka to Chittagong are empty (see Box 2.2).

For a number of commodity routes, such as bulk cargoes between India and Bangladesh and transit cargo from Nepal, rail has a competitive advantage. The establishment of a dual-gauge rail link across the Jamuna Bridge is expected to provide a significant increase in containers once the broad-gauge connection is extended to Dhaka. The principal rail routes under consider-

after being above 50 percent in the early 1980s in terms of ton-kilometers, dropped below 40 percent by 1992 and continued to decline thereafter, although tonnage has recently increased.[6] The factors leading to the loss in market share include low operating speeds (15 kilometers per hour or less), shortages of equipment, especially locomotives, poor track conditions, and long and unpredictable delays. Rail transport is also relatively expensive because of the inefficiency of

_____
6. *India Transport Sector Report 13192-N*, World Bank, 1995.

ation are the broad-gauge routes connecting East India with west Bangladesh (at the Benapole-Petrapole, Darshan-Gede, and Radhikapur-Birol border crossings) from Tripura through Maishassan to Shahbajpur and on to Sylhet. A more complete discussion of Bangladesh Railways and links with Indian Railways is provided in Background Note 3.

A protocol exists for the interchange of rail wagons across the India-Bangladesh border. It sets out the charges for the exchange of wagons and establishes a target wagon balance. Rail track does not appear to create a physical constraint for the movement of trains across the border, but Indian and Bangladeshi wagons have different coupling and braking systems that restrict operating speeds for Indian trains hauling Bangladeshi cars. The freight trains in India are typically 40 wagons in length, whereas those in Bangladesh are 35 wagons long. The Indian trains must be broken into two sections, with the second section waiting for up to a week for another locomotive. Since the rakes traveling from Bangladesh to India usually carry consignments for a variety of locations, the wagons must be reassigned to other trains shortly after passing into India. About 2,000 Indian wagons in transit through Bangladesh have been "lost" over the last decade.

Inland Water Transport

Bangladesh has an extensive inland water network that links with West Bengal on its west and Assam and Northeast India on the east. The Class I routes operate throughout the year with a minimum draft of 12 feet. However, shifting rivers, increasing levels of siltation, and a lowering of groundwater due to pumping have made it difficult to maintain the depths on the secondary routes. Furthermore, the old and inefficient dredging fleet and limited hydrographic survey prevent the routes from being properly maintained.

BOX 2.2   CONTAINER TRAFFIC MOVEMENT BETWEEN CHITTAGONG AND DHAKA

Chittagong port handles 95 percent of the total containers received in Bangladesh, and 85 to 90 percent of these are bound for Dhaka. However, only 10 to 12 percent (less than 40,000 ton equivalent units are moved by rail to an inland container depot (ICD). Dhaka has a capacity of 100,000 ton equivalent units. The remaining container traffic (90 percent) is unpacked at Chittagong and moved in break bulk by small trucks. There is no container movement by road due to axle load limitation on bridges. The reason for this anomaly is the rail charges and regulations between Chittagong and Dhaka. A shipper who books a container for delivery to Dhaka ICD has to pay the shipping line an extra US$350 for a 20-foot container or US$550 for a 40-foot container for Chittagong-Dhaka movement by rail. Of this, Bangladesh Railway charges only US$120 to US$180 for a 20-foot container, depending on the quantity of cargo, and US$200 for a 40-foot container. Bangladesh Railway does not guarantee the safety of goods on this route, and the shipping line justifies this extra charge as coverage for damage. The truckers, however, charge US$80 to US$100 for an amount of break-bulk cargo equivalent to a 20-foot container load. Since the difference is substantial, the shippers and exporters prefer to move goods in break bulk and unload or load at Chittagong port. This causes congestion at the port as well as on the Dhaka-Chittagong road. Also, this is not the safest way of handling the container cargo. If Bangladesh Railway were to provide cargo insurance as part of its tariff, substantial container traffic could get diverted to rail. This would benefit the shipper as well as the port and railway. The congestion at the port would be reduced, the turnaround would improve, and there would be better utilization of available space at Dhaka ICD.

So far, the government has not been able to dedicate the resources necessary to maintain either a complete network of primary and secondary routes or the navigational markers needed to allow nighttime operations on all the primary routes.

India and Bangladesh have well-developed private sector barge operations. The barge fleets include both self-propelled and dumb barges that are 10 to 15 years old. The capacity ranges from 150 tons for self-propelled and up to 1,200 tons for dumb barges (see Background Note 5). There is a significant overcapacity, which has led to strong competition and low freight rates but limited consolidation. Most operators continue to own a single barge or a small fleet. The inland water transport has the lowest charges per ton-kilometer freight transport for cargoes with origins and destinations near the rivers. It loses cost advantage when trucks are required to move cargo to and from the rivers.

Bangladesh and India signed an Inland Water Transport transit protocol in 1980. The protocol allowed Indian barges to transit Bangladesh between West Bengal and Northeast India, but it prohibited transshipment of Bangladeshi cargo en route. In October 1999, a revised protocol was introduced that allows Indian barges to transport cargo between the two countries, provided that both countries share the transportation of cross-border trade and transit cargo on an equal tonnage basis. Despite low costs and the absence of cross-border transshipment requirements, inland waterway transport is at a competitive disadvantage because of its low travel speeds, which average less than 50 kilometers per day due to the limitations on night navigation and physical constraints on routes. Despite these limitations, the Bangladeshi private sector is seeking to capture additional regional traffic, including the petroleum products shipped from the Numaligarh

refinery in Assam to markets in Bangladesh and West Bengal.

International Shipping

The fourth mode of transport is ocean shipping through Calcutta and Chittagong ports. These ports are positioned well north of the main shipping lines and handle relatively small volumes of cargo. As a result they attract relatively old and inefficient vessels. The container vessels are feeder ships of up to 750 TEU (20 foot equivalent unit) and bulk vessels of 25,000 dead weight tonnage (dwt) or less.

Containers are transshipped via Singapore or Colombo. Feeder services are provided by independent operators that transport boxes for several large container lines. The time required for the feeder movement and transshipment is about eight days—three days of sailing time and five days in the transshipment port waiting for the mother vessel. Table 2.5 shows typical container freight rates and shipping times for the sample of routes under study.

The situation for noncontainerized general cargo is somewhat different. The amount and frequency of general cargo liner services has been declining steadily. These have been replaced by container liner services and by chartered vessels carrying neo-bulk cargo. For large shipments of neo-bulk cargoes, the cost of ocean transport is dependent on the size of the vessel. This is determined by the depth of the port as well as the size of typical consignments. The draft limitations at Calcutta, Haldia, Chittagong, and Mongla are 7.5, 8.4, 9, and 4 (7.5 at anchorage) meters, respectively. The routing of neo-bulk cargoes is generally determined by the availability of railroad and inland water access to the port having adequate depth.

The protocols for handling transit cargo from other countries appear to be well established for

TABLE 2.5   SAMPLE OCEAN FREIGHT CHARACTERISTICS

Route	Cargo	Rate/TEU[a] (US$)	Days
New Zealand-Calcutta	Wool	1,200	24
Calcutta-WCUS	Garments	3,100	35
Chittagong/Calcutta-U.K.	Tea	1,250	23.5
Singapore-Chittagong/Calcutta	Polypropylene	975	10
Calcutta-Germany	Carpets	1,200	22

a. 20 foot equivalent unit.
Source: Logistics cost study team, World Bank.

these ports. The principal barriers to efficient transfer are the slow handling rates, restrictive labor practices, poor operational controls, and cumbersome customs procedures. Bangladesh is currently implementing a preshipment inspection and valuation for selected imports at their port of origin in order to reduce the time required for customs inspection. Although this should improve transparency and reduce informal payments, it will not significantly reduce the time required for customs clearance because many of the delays are associated with the preparation of customs documents and inspections.

Border Crossings

There are three types of border crossings: road, rail, and seaports (Table 2.6). The road crossings consist of a customs checkpoint for vehicles moving across the border, a truck waiting area, and an area for cargo inspection. Where cargo must be transshipped, additional space must be provided for storing cargo and for unloading and loading trucks. The rail crossings consist of sidings or rail yards where locomotives are exchanged from those of one country to those of the next. No storage is required because the cargo remains in the rail cars rather than being transferred. The seaports provide a full range of services, including loading and unloading facilities, vehicle fleeting areas, and cargo storage and consolidation, as well as transfer to and from ocean transport.

Currently the transit protocols limit not only the border crossings but also the number of routes that can be used for transporting cargo. Some of the protocols require that the cargo be transshipped from the vehicles of one country to those of another, which increases not only the time and cost for transport but also the damage to the cargo and the variance in travel time. These problems could be reduced if cargo were allowed to move in-bond (meaning that the containerized

TABLE 2.6   MAJOR BORDER CROSSINGS

Border	Crossing Points	Modes
Nepal/India	Birgunj/Raxaul	Road, Rail[a]
	Biratnagar/Jogbani	Road
	Bhairahawa/Nautanwa	Road
	Kakarvitta/Phulbari	Road
	Nepalganj	Road
Bhutan/India	Phutsoling-Jaigaon	Road
Bangladesh/India	Benapole/Petrapole	Road, Rail[a]
	Darshana/Gede	Rail BG[b]
	Rohanpur/Singhebad	Rail BG[b]
	Birol/Radihkapur	Rail MG[c]
	Shahbajpur/Mahishasan	Rail MG[c]
	Banglbandha /Phulbari	Road
	Chilhati/Haldibari	Rail (potential)
	Burimari/Changra bandha	Road
	Hili/ Balurghat	Road
	Tamabil/Daukii	Road
	Karimganj/Zakiganj	Road
	Sonamasjid/	Road
	Akhaura/ Agartala	Road, Rail[d]
India/	Calcutta	Ocean
	Haldia	Ocean
Bangladesh	Chittagong	Ocean

a. Operational by 2001.
b. Broad gauge.
c. Meter gauge.
d. Planned.
Source: Background Notes 3 and 6.

cargoes could remain in the sealed container box even when the cargo has to be transshipped) with ICDs and other facilities established at the border to expedite movement across the border. The regional border crossings vary in their level of development. The crossing at Benapole is the most developed. It has warehousing, parking areas, and a well-developed market with logistics services. Despite all these facilities, Benapole suffers from severe congestion, and cargo must be diverted to other crossings (see Box 2.3).

The facilities at the Birol, Hili, Sonamasjid Rohanpur, and Burimari border crossings are much simpler. The crossings have customs facilities and roadside parking, but they lack truck

unloading ramps, warehouses, telecommunications, and other logistics services. Among the least-developed crossings is the Phulbari corridor linking Kakariatha, Nepal via India to Banglabandh, Bangladesh. The Banglabandh crossing lacks even basic customs facilities. Table 2.7 provides information on problems at major border crossings.

For transit cargo between India and Nepal, three border point ICDs are being constructed to expedite handling and storage.[7] These are intended to provide efficient transfer of containers on trucks or, in the case of Birgunj, on rail cars. The Birgunj ICD will be equipped with reach stackers to allow efficient transshipment of cargo between trucks and between rail and truck.

As Table 2.8 shows, customs clearance procedures can add significant costs and delays even though they represent a relatively small part of the logistics chain. The existing procedures are both cumbersome and time-consuming, and they reflect the conservative trade policies that have characterized the region for decades. Poorly defined or complex procedures and documents reduce transparency, especially where a large number of people are required to give approvals.

Table 2.9 shows the documents that are submitted to customs at the border crossings. Many are the same as those commonly required at other international borders, such as invoices, packing lists, certificates of origin, letters of credit, and quarantine forms for plants and foods. Some of the documents, such as import licenses, export permits, and various certificates, are less common. These are intended to meet local requirements. They supply information that should already be available to the customs officials and

---

BOX 2.3   BENAPOLE: BOTTLENECK AT THE INDIAN-BANGLADESH BORDER

Benapole is the principal border crossing between India and Bangladesh. The facility is called a land port: its functions are limited to providing a customs checkpoint and bonded warehouses. It has a large number of clearing agents who maintain offices on the site, and there are adequate telecommunication services. Import traffic for Bangladesh is transferred from Indian trucks to bonded facilities within Bangladesh while export traffic is transshipped into warehouses 500 meters inside the Indian border. The average daily traffic exceeds 200 trucks loaded with cargo for Bangladesh and 50 trucks with cargo for India, as well as 2,000 passengers. Throughput is constrained by a single customs lane in each direction for clearing vehicles and emigrants. As a result, there is severe congestion with lines of up to 1,500 trucks and waiting times of one to five days. The area has a large complex of warehouses and markets, but it is constrained by a narrow road leading to the border and a lack of parking spaces. The area in Benapole for transshipping goods from Indian trucks to Bangladeshi trucks can accommodate only 250 to 300 trucks. Customs procedures are largely to blame for the delays, with normal customs working hours limited to 9 a.m. to 6 p.m. The congestion has reached such a level that traffic has been diverted to more remote border crossings where there is less rigorous enforcement of customs inspections.

The facility also has operational problems. The 30-plus warehouses provided by the Mongla Port Authority have adequate capacity (about 15,000 tons), but there is low utilization due to poor maintenance, difficult access, inadequate security, and no running water or sanitary facilities. The facility lacks adequate cargo handling equipment. Cranes are in poor condition. There are no inland container depots and no provision for receiving and delivering cargo to shipping lines.

In order to reduce congestion, a new truck terminal has been constructed in Benapole, in addition to a bypass road leading to the crossing. On the Indian side, a parking area for 400 to 500 trucks is being constructed, in addition to new private warehousing. However, the more important issues related to simplifying customs procedures, eliminating the need for transshipment, and increasing private sector involvement in operations have yet to be addressed.

---

7. The World Bank assisted "Nepal Multimodal Transport and Trade Facilitation Project."

not submitted with each shipment. Other documents, such as equipment interchange certificates for containers and railway cars and registration forms for vehicles and drivers moving across the border, are required because simplified procedures for in-bond movements and modern regulations for the carriage of goods have yet to be developed.

The basic customs documents, such as transit, export, and import declarations, create problems because they vary from country to country and must be prepared separately for each side of the border and submitted in multiple copies. A standardized format would not only reduce the paperwork but also encourage more consistent procedures and greater coordination between customs officials on either side of the border. The problem of standardization has been hampered by India's decision to develop a separate trade classification system while its neighbors adopted the ASYCUDA automated systems format.

The document problem is not limited to the number of documents that must be submitted, but also includes the procedures used for verifying and approving documents. The number of copies that must be submitted and, more importantly, the number of signatures required, add considerably to the cost. Although the requirements for the Nepal–India movements have been reduced in the last few years, considerable improvements are still needed.

Ports

The ports represent the critical border crossing in terms of costs and time. The time the cargo spends in port is determined by four factors: the complexity of the customs clearance procedures, the frequency of vessel arrivals, the efficiency of the cargo handling and storage operations, and the efficiency of the shippers and consignees. The latter depends on the level of coordination

TABLE 2.7 CHARACTERISTICS OF MAJOR BORDER CROSSINGS

Border crossing	Mode	Problems
Chittagong	Water	Inefficient management and operations, lack of equipment, excessive delays and costs
Calcutta	Water	Inefficient management and operations, lack of equipment, excessive delays and costs
Benapole/Petrapol	Road	Congestion
Birgunj/Rauxal	Rail	ICD not yet operational
Bhairahwa/Notanawa	Road	ICD not yet operational
Biratnagar/ Jogbani	Road	ICD not yet operational
Darsana/Gede	Rail	Long processing times
Kakarbhitta-Panitanki	Road	Poor facilities on both borders, no customs office at Banglaband
Burimari-Changrabaandh	Road	Insufficient infrastructure, lack of customs office, bad road access

Source: Background Notes 6, 7, 8, and 9.

TABLE 2.8 COSTS AND TIME FOR CUSTOMS INSPECTION AND CLEARANCE

Mode	Commodity	US$/ton	Time (hrs)
Regional			
Barge	Cement	0.07	24
Truck	Agricultural produce	16.24	30
Truck	Limestone	6.05	32.5
Truck/ferry	Yarn	6.55	205
International			
Truck	Wool	8.94	63
Truck	Tea	14.29	12
Truck	Carpet	27.00	20
Truck	Polypropylene	6.54	55
Truck	Cotton garment	5.94	36

Source: Logistics cost study, World Bank.

TABLE 2.9   BORDER CROSSING DOCUMENTATION

Cargo routes	Documents required
India to Bangladesh Import Cargo	For Indian customs—Customs export declaration, bill of lading, invoice, packing list, letter of credit. For Bangladeshi customs—Import permit, bill of lading, packing list, letter of credit, consignment insurance cover, certificate of registration (value-added tax), importer pass book. For goods entering the export-process zone—Bonded warehouse licenses, value-bonded form, risk and duty bond.
Nepal to India Transit Cargo	For Nepali customs —Customs transit declaration, customs export declaration, duty insurance certificate, invoice, packing list, certificate of origin, certificates of registration (income tax, value-added tax, company), letter of credit. For Indian customs—Customs transit document, duty insurance, invoice, packing list, letter of credit, certificate of origin.
Bangladesh to Nepal	For Bangladeshi customs—Export registration certificate, invoice, letter of credit, packing list, certificate of origin, truck receipt. For Nepali customs—Customs import declaration, invoice, packing list, certificate of origin, import license, letter of credit, health/quarantine certificate, equipment interchange receipt, and duty insurance coverage for containers.
Bangladesh Ports	Exports—Export bill of entry, invoice, packing list, export permit, undertaking by export company, outpass statement, export permit, risk bond.
India Ports	Imports—Customs transit declaration, bill of lading, invoice, packing list, certificate of origin , import license, letter of credit, health/quarantine certificate , equipment interchange receipt and duty insurance coverage for containers.

Source: Background Notes 8 and 9.

in processing shipping documents and the ability of the shipper and consignee to time shipments so as not to use the port for storing inventory to be sold. There are significant problems with all four components that cause the relatively long time delays for cargo in port.

For import and export cargoes, the effectiveness of a route is very much dependent on the port services. The time and cost for oceanborne transport generally exceeds the time for land transport even where the latter involves a long distance. In many situations the longer land route is preferable because it provides access to a larger, more efficient port that has better connections to foreign origins and destinations. The South Asia ports can be grouped into three levels of service. At the highest level are major transshipment hubs that have frequent sailings by large shipping lines offering scheduled services to different regions of the world. These services typically operate on a day-of-the-week schedule so that importers and exporters can time their shipments to minimize the time in port. The only major transshipment hub in the immediate region is Colombo. It has obtained this status by virtue of its proximity to the major markets of South Asia, its location along the equatorial routing of the larger liner services, and its efficiency relative to the ports in southern India. The other transshipment ports serving the region are Singapore, which handles most of the feeder services to Chittagong and Calcutta, and Dubai/Aden, which serves the west coast of India.

The second level of ports are regional hub ports such as Nhava Sheva and Port Kelang. Although located away from the major shipping routes, they have day-of-the-week calls by major shipping lines that have a portion of their voyages call at these ports.[8] The number of regional hubs will increase with the growth in traffic. The Thai port of Laem Chabang is approaching hub status, and there is likely to be a regional hub on the east coast of India during this decade.

The third category of ports are regional seaports such as Calcutta, Chittagong, and Haldia. These attract feeder services from the major transshipment hubs that operate on a flexible schedule, so it is difficult to schedule cargo movements to connect with major shipping lines. This introduces delays at both the feeder port and the transshipment port. It also creates an additional cost for a second handling. The smaller feeder vessels have higher operating costs per unit of cargo, but this additional cost is lower than the

cost of the larger vessels calling at the port to transfer relatively small cargo loads. Economically, they are able to provide more frequent service to the transshipment hubs.

The status of Chittagong, Calcutta, and Haldia as feeder ports is unlikely to change because of limitations on the volume of cargoes, their distance from the main shipping routes, and their low cargo handling productivity. Chittagong has no container gantry cranes. This, together with labor problems, reduces the handling productivity below five containers per vessel-hour. In addition, vessels are forced to wait for berths for two to seven days. Total turnaround time can range from five to thirteen days for an activity that would require less than one day in most ports. The performance in Calcutta and Haldia is not much better.[9] If a new, privately operated port were developed in Patenga, Bangladesh, or along the east coast of India, it should be able to divert substantial traffic from existing public ports and generate some additional traffic—which has happened at the Jawaharlal Nehru Port Trust on the west coast of India.[10] However, it would be unlikely to achieve regional port status because of the limited import-export traffic generated by the region.

Improvements in port performance through faster, more reliable equipment and better management of labor will increase berth productivity and reduce delays to vessels. If this were combined with guaranteed availability of berth space, day-of-the-week sailings could be introduced. At

---

8. Large container shipping lines and alliances serving major routes increasingly operate with variations of their main route called strings. Each voyage or string will call at a certain number of secondary ports as well as the main ports.

9. For additional discussion of impediments to port efficiency, see Background Notes 8 and 9.

10. The success of private port operations in improving productivity, diverting traffic from public ports, and attracting new traffic is well documented. Examples include Laem Chabang in Thailand, Giao Tauro in Italy, Manzanillo in Panama, and Nhava Sheva in India.

present, any attempt to introduce a fixed schedule would require excessive slack time in the sailing schedule because of the uncertainties in port performance and would result in inefficient use of vessels. This is a common problem in regions with underdeveloped ports, such as Southeast Asia and the east coast of South America, but there are attempts to overcome this problem through investments in modern cargo-handling equipment and privatization of port operations. The results have been a significant reduction in port costs, freight rates, and times for ocean shipment.

ANALYSIS OF LOGISTICS COSTS AND TIMES

The times and costs for moving cargo along the 11 routes listed in Table 2.1 were estimated from information provided by cargo owners and forwarders based on typical shipments. We analyzed the information to determine the relative contributions of the various logistics activities as follows:

- Loading at the origin and unloading at the destination,

- Line-haul movements,

- Intermediate handling at the border crossings and ports, and

- Customs inspections.

The analysis included the land movement and the transfer across the border through the seaport, but it did not include ocean transport.

Table 2.10 summarizes the costs for the individual activities. The costs for initial loading and final unloading and the intermediate cargo handling were computed per ton of cargo handled, and the line-haul transport was computed per

ton-kilometer to take account of differences in vehicle size and mode. For truck transport, an additional calculation was made for the charges per kilometer. For loading the cargo at its origin and unloading at its destination, the costs differ from less than US$1 per ton to over US$25.[11] The higher costs were due to the packaging requirements of higher value cargoes, specifically textiles, tea, and freight of all kinds (FAK). Since wool and polypropylene are imports, the packaging was performed at foreign origins (New Zealand and Singapore), and these charges are not included in the table.

The cost for the line-haul movement depends on the mode. The rates for rail and barge transport were lower than for trucking when calculated on a per ton-kilometer basis. For trucking, the rates range from US$0.029–US$0.058 per ton-kilometer, depending on the size of the shipments and whether the trip is short distance or long distance. Limestone, tea, and FAK were carried in eight-ton loads, whereas the other cargoes have consignments about twice that size. The rate per truck-kilometer was relatively consistent, between US$0.45 and US$0.50, except for agricultural products, which had an exceptionally low rate for movement to the border crossing at Kakarbhitta. These rates are significantly higher than the estimated trucking costs presented in Table 2.3. This is because of fewer-than-expected backhauls, increased delays en route, and the informal costs paid at various police checkpoints.

Intermediate handling occurs where there is transshipment between vehicles, a change in cargo form, or a transfer of cargo to and from storage and from one mode to another. The amounts paid ranged from US$1.6 per ton to over US$31.

---

11. These costs do not include the cost of time.

TABLE 2.10   UNIT COSTS FOR MOVEMENT OF CARGO BY ROUTE AND COMMODITY

Origin/destination	Mode	Cargo	Initial load and final unload (US$/ton)	Line haul[a] (US$/ ton-km)	(US$/km)	Intermediate handling[b] (US$/ton)	Customs procedures[c] (% value)
Domestic							
1 Calcutta-Argatala	Rail	Cement	0.46	0.016	n.a.	n.a.	n.a.
2 Calcutta-Siliguri-Argatala	Truck	Freight, all kinds	34.75	0.059	0.47	n.a.	n.a.
Regional							
3 Calcutta-Sheikhbaria-Argatala	Barge	Cement	0.46	0.022	n.a.	1.60	0.11
4 Kathmandu-Kakarbhitta-Dhaka	Truck	Ag. produce	3.88	0.033	0.28	4.24	4.60
5 Thimpu-Jaigon-Burimari-Dhaka	Truck	Limestone	3.33	0.058	0.43	4.80	12.11
6 Calcutta-Benapole-Dhaka	Truck/ferry	Yarn	35.47	0.097	n.a.	5.41	0.26
International							
7 NewZealand -Calcutta-Raxaul-Kathmandu	Truck	Wool	2.35	0.044	0.37[b]	25.82	0.45
8 Karimganj-Siliguri-Calcutta-Liverpool	Truck	Tea	28.57	0.053	0.45	27.38	0.60
9 Kathmandu-Raxaul-Calcutta-Bremen	Truck/rail	Carpet	18.33	0.031	0.47	16.40	0.45
10 Singapore-Calcutta-Jaigon-Thimpu	Truck	Polypropylene	1.56	0.031	0.50	31.31	1.28
11 Dhaka-Chittagong-west coast of the United States	Truck	Cotton garments	20.56	0.029	0.46	10.38	0.20

a. Charges for movements by truck, rail, or barge.
b. Transshipment of cargo at border crossings, packing and unpacking of containers, and other handling of cargo in port.
c. Formal and informal charges for cargo clearance and inspection.
d. Assumes that two trucks are required for 17 tons because of high volume.
n.a. = Not available.
Source: Logistics costs study, World Bank.

These amounts were less a function of the value of the cargo and more a function of the number and type of border crossings involved.

Customs clearance procedures, exclusive of duties, accounted for less than 0.5 percent of the cargo value for most of the routes. The percentages varied inversely with the value of the cargo, indicating that a significant part of these costs are related less to the value of the cargo than to the volume of cargo. The major exceptions are the agricultural products, which incur an extremely high cost for the customs procedures at Phulbari (Map 3).

The costs for these different components were compared as a proportion of the total costs for the different logistics activities (see Figures 2.1 and 2.2). This comparison does not include the charges for handling at the origin and destination because these are imputed costs based on the time spent by regular employees in the production process.[13] When this cost is excluded, the line-haul costs should account for at least 85 percent of the total for regional shipments and at least 75 percent for foreign shipments with the exception of short distances. For the first three routes (regional routes 3 to 5), the cost for line-haul transport was dominant. However, for the shipment of agricultural products, the other costs were more than one-third of the total because of the relatively high costs for customs clearance in crossing from the Nepali and Bangladeshi borders.[12]

For the international routes, (Routes 7 to 11 in Table 2.10), the costs other than line haul account for 40 to 60 percent. Customs procedures were significant in both Calcutta and Chittagong ports because of inefficiencies and informal payments. The costs for intermediate handling were about 20 to 25 percent of total costs because they included all handling costs in port other than loading and unloading the vessel. These numbers are reasonable except in the case of polypropylene offloaded in Calcutta, which incurred exceptionally high costs for handling and storage.

Customs clearance procedures add a relatively small amount to the logistics costs with the exception of agricultural products, which incurred high costs at Phulbari customs, and carpets, which experienced high formal and informal fees at Raxaul and Calcutta. The costs for customs procedures are not significant when compared to the value of the cargo, as shown in Table 2.10. The exceptions are agricultural produce, as mentioned above, and limestone, which has a very low product value. Overall the customs procedures had a greater impact on delays than on costs.

The time spent on individual components of the logistics chain is influenced by a number of factors. For example, the time spent loading at the point of production is more dependent on production schedules than on the productivity of the physical handling. Figure 2.1, which excludes this component, shows the relative importance of the remaining logistics activities. With reasonably efficient operations, it should be expected that line-haul movements would account for 80 to 90 percent of the time for regional movements and 75 to 80 percent of the total time for international movements for all but the shortest routes. In fact the percentages are much lower due to inefficiencies at the border crossings.

For the regional routes, the line haul accounts for 57 to 65 percent of the logistics time, exclusive of loading and unloading at the origin and destination. Customs procedures account for most of the additional time on the routes from Bhutan and Nepal to Dhaka. These routes require two border crossings and one transshipment, with the majority of the time lost in clearing the cargo through customs. The movement of cement by barge does not involve significant border checks, but it does require transfers to trucks at both ends, which adds a significant amount of time.

The international routes require a lot of time in port. This includes time spent clearing customs, but it is primarily the time spent waiting to enter the port, loading and unloading the vessel, and in storage waiting for the vessel. The proportion is greatest for Route 11 because of the

---

12. There are also significant costs for damages that have not been included.

short travel time between Chittagong and Dhaka. Although the movement of polypropylene is much longer, the exceptionally long delay in the port of Calcutta accounts for a large part of the logistics costs.

The last route, the domestic shipment of yarn from Calcutta to Dhaka, highlights the extremely long waiting times for customs at Benapole. Table 2.7 shows the times associated with customs processing on both sides of the border. The delays at crossings other than Benapole appear to be, if not justifiable, at least manageable.

As Table 2.11 shows, overall route performance can be compared using two performance measures: average speed and unit cost. The average speed of the journey compares the land route distance and travel time for the line-haul movement. The unit cost for the journey is equal to the logistics costs for the land movement divided by the product of the route distance and consignment size (for example, $/ton-kilometer).

The average speed was less than 400 kilometers per day because of the congestion on the roads and the delays en route for the railway. The speeds are higher in Bangladesh because there is less traffic congestion. The cost per ton-kilometer is lowest for all-rail and all-barge shipments and highest for short-distance truck movements.

Four general conclusions can be drawn from this route comparison. The first is that the overall logistics costs, although significant for some commodities, is not all that great when measured as a percentage of cargo value. The inefficiencies of the transport services are offset by low labor costs and older, fully depreciated transport equipment. As a result these percentages are comparable with those experienced elsewhere. The problem is not the cost but rather the time, reliability, and safety of the logistics services.

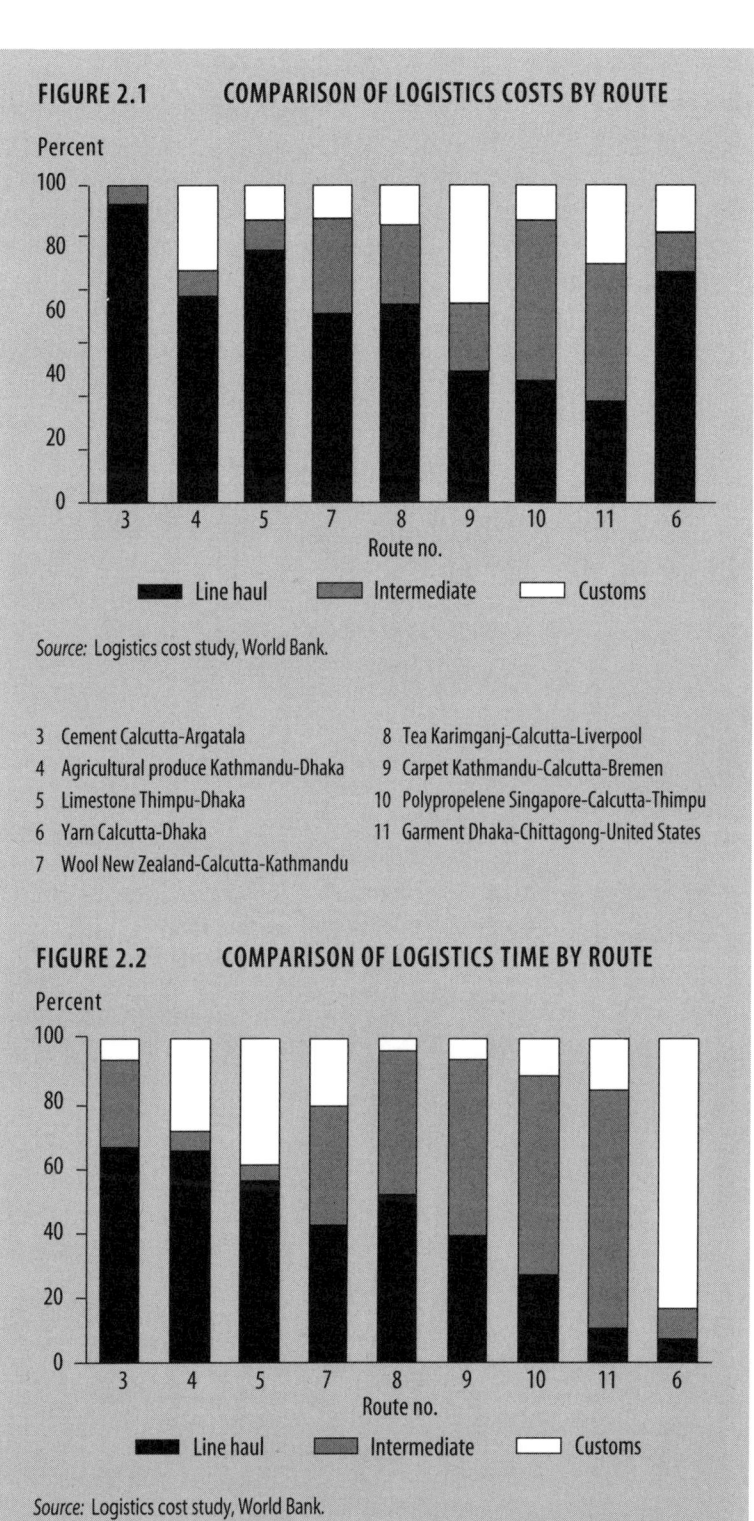

FIGURE 2.1   COMPARISON OF LOGISTICS COSTS BY ROUTE

Percent

Line haul   Intermediate   Customs

Source: Logistics cost study, World Bank.

3 Cement Calcutta-Argatala
4 Agricultural produce Kathmandu-Dhaka
5 Limestone Thimpu-Dhaka
6 Yarn Calcutta-Dhaka
7 Wool New Zealand-Calcutta-Kathmandu
8 Tea Karimganj-Calcutta-Liverpool
9 Carpet Kathmandu-Calcutta-Bremen
10 Polypropelene Singapore-Calcutta-Thimpu
11 Garment Dhaka-Chittagong-United States

FIGURE 2.2   COMPARISON OF LOGISTICS TIME BY ROUTE

Percent

Line haul   Intermediate   Customs

Source: Logistics cost study, World Bank.

TABLE 2.11   BASIC COMPARATIVE PERFORMANCE MEASURES

Route	Mode	Cargo	Km/day	US$/ton-km
Calcutta-Agartala	Rail	Cement	818	0.02
Calcutta-Agartala	Truck	Freight, all kinds	216	0.08
Calcutta-Agartala	Barge	Cement	154	0.02
Kathmandu-Dhaka	Truck	Agricultural produce	415	0.05
Thimpu-Dhaka	Truck	Limestone	401	0.08
New Zealand-Calcutta-Kathmandu	Truck	Wool	228	0.07
Karimganj-Calcutta-Liverpool	Truck	Tea	197	0.10
Kathmandu-Calcutta-Bremen	Truck/rail	Carpet	211	0.09
Singapore-Calcutta-Thimpu	Truck	Polypropylene	158	0.08
Dhaka-Chittagong-United States	Truck	Cotton garments	281	0.16
Calcutta-Dhaka	Truck	Yarn	506	0.23

Source: Consultant study team estimates.

The second conclusion is that the border crossings are a major cause of higher costs and longer delivery times. The critical bottlenecks are the seaports, the Benapole crossing, and the Nepal border crossings. The problems at the crossings are being addressed through the provision of additional infrastructure. They are also being addressed through changes at procedures at the Nepal border crossings.

The third is that the customs clearance procedures are a problem in terms of unnecessary delays and unofficial costs. However, they do not have as great an impact as other procedures at the border crossings and ports. Customs can and should be more efficient, but the protocols are the major source of inefficiency. Customs limitation on working hours, supply of officials at the crossing, the number of gates for receiving cargo, and the transparency of procedures for inspection and valuation not only reduce efficiency but also generate animosity. More im-

portantly, they create uncertainty concerning the delivery time for and condition of the cargo.

The fourth conclusion is that the priority should be given to improving procedures in the short term and infrastructure in the medium term.

The border crossings can add considerable uncertainty to the time involved and damage incurred in transporting the cargo; especially where border-crossing procedures are complex or require frequent inspections. Manufactured products are increasingly sensitive to this problem because tighter logistics are required in modern commerce. The inability to guarantee delivery schedules requires the recipient of the cargo to maintain extra inventory to prevent a shortfall due to late deliveries. The inability to guarantee the condition of the cargo adds to the cost for insurance and makes it more difficult to sell the product. Variances in the costs for crossing the border place the profitability of shipments in jeopardy. The product price must be increased to take into account the upper range of costs.

IMPLICATIONS OF LOGISTICS CONSTRAINTS AND CHARACTERISTICS OF GOODS

The efficiency and effectiveness of different routes depend on both the characteristics of the route and the nature of the cargo being moved. Cargo is typically characterized as break bulk, unitized, neo-bulk, or bulk. Each requires specialized handling systems if the goods have to compete effectively for market share. The type of cargo and the markets in which it is sold determine the type of logistics services required to compete effectively for market share. The important cargo characteristics include:

- The value of the cargo per unit volume or weight,

- The susceptibility of the cargo to damage while in transit and when handled, and

- The physical and commercial life of the cargo.

The third item has both physical and commercial dimensions, as Chapter 1 discussed. Some commodities—most notably, fruits and vegetables—have a relatively short physical life. Others have a short commercial life. For example, garments and footwear are affected by changes in season and fashion.

The competitiveness of the markets in which the cargo is sold also affects the logistics requirements. Market sensitivity to the delivery times and variations in those delivery times, as well as to delivery costs and variations in those costs, are particularly important.

These sets of characteristics are linked. The first item is linked to the delivered cost where that cost is measured relative to value of the cargo. The second item is also linked to the delivered cost because damages or losses during transit increase the delivered that cost. The third item is linked to the delivery time because it limits the acceptable time for delivery. Table 2.12 shows the relationship between the physical and commercial characteristics of the cargo and the type of logistics required.

Commodities can be categorized according to the level of logistics services required. The first category is high-value, time-sensitive cargoes that are vulnerable to damage. These must be moved quickly, generally in unitized form, with a minimum amount of transfers. Typical reorder times are 1.5 to 2 months, implying a maximum travel time of 25 to 35 days. The price of transport is less important than the time and reliability of deliveries. Higher-value cargo can afford a higher cost of transport. Among the cargoes in this category are fruits and vegetables, meat, fish (both fresh and frozen), and other food products. The shipper chooses the fastest mode of transport with a preference for the route that has the least number of handlings. Road transport is generally preferred unless transshipment can be avoided through the use of rail transport. For high-valued perishables, air freight is preferred.

Four other commodities—consumer goods, wood products, seasonal garments, and textiles—are often included in the first group. These can be divided between upscale products such as electronics, fashion garments, and designer furniture that have a shorter shelf life and tight delivery schedules, and low-cost products such as appliances, basic clothes, and general furniture that tend to have a longer shelf life and much looser delivery schedules.

These low-cost goods are part of the second category: medium-value commodities with

TABLE 2.12   COMMODITY CHARACTERISTICS

Commodity	Value US$/ton	Density[a]	Shelf life Physical[b]	Shelf life Commercial[c]	Susceptibility damage and loss[d]	Market sensitivity Delivered cost[e]	Market sensitivity Delivery time[e]
Fruits and vegetables	1,500	M	S	S	V	M	V
Fresh meat and fish	2,000	M	S	S	V	V	V
Frozen meat and fish	3,000	M	M	S	V	M	V
Tea	2,400	L	M	M	M	M	M
Grain	200	M	L	L	M	V	M
Jute, cotton		L	L	L	M	V	M
Textiles, fabric, yarn	2,500	L	L	M	M	V	V
Carpets	6,000	L	L	L	M	M	M
Garments	3,000	L	L	M	M	V	V
Wood products	1,500	L	L	M	M	V	M
Food products	1,500	M	M	M	M	M	V
Consumer goods	2,500	L	M	M	M	V	M
Cement	60	H	M	L	M	V	M
Clinker	< 50	H	L	L	N	V	M
Timber	500	M	L	M	M	M	M
Steel products	350	H	L	L	N	V	M
Petroleum and oil products	200	H	L	M	N	V	M
Petrochemicals	500	H	L	M	N	M	V

Notes:
a. L = low (< 0.7), M = medium, H = high (≥ 1.0).
b. S = short (< 1 month), M = moderate, L = long (> 1 year).
c. S = short (< 3 months), M = moderate, L = long (> 9 months)
d. V = very susceptible, M = moderately susceptible, N = relatively impervious.
e. V = very sensitive, M = moderately sensitive, N = relatively insensitive.
Source: Consultant study team estimates.

moderate shelf lives and limited susceptibility to damage. Carpets are included in this group despite their high value. They are only moderately susceptible to damage and, most important, have a long shelf life. Other commodities in this group are jute, cotton and other fibers, tea, timber, and petrochemicals. Delivery times are longer, about forty to sixty days. Reorder times are two to three months. These commodities are more price sensitive, so it is necessary to select logistics services that balance between cost and time. Trucking is preferred, but the shipper may choose rail or inland water if it provides a lower cost and fewer handlings.

The remaining category includes low-value commodities with long shelf lives that are relatively impervious to loss or damage. These are typically bulk cargoes such as grains, cement, and limestone. Their logistics emphasize low-cost, reliable transport. Because these commodities tend to be handled in large volumes, the logistics are less concerned with minimizing delivery time and more with maintaining a reliable delivery schedule. The greater the variance in delivery times, the larger the inventories that must be maintained to avoid outages. The shipper will prefer the mode that handles large consignments but minimizes the number of handlings. Rail is the most popular mode, followed by inland water transport. Where these are not readily available, road transport will be used, especially for petroleum products.

For all three groups, there will be a preference for routes that do not require border crossings with significant delays or transshipments. Table 2.13 shows the impact of the logistics costs on the delivered cost of the cargo. These logistics costs, including the ocean freight for imports and exports, are divided by the delivered cost of the cargo. Not surprisingly, the percentage is greatest for the low-value cargoes, such as cement and limestone, and least for the high-value cargoes, such as carpets, garments, yarn, and con-

sumer goods. The cargo value has a greater impact than the distance shipped, as can be seen by comparing the local shipment of agricultural products with the export of cotton garments to the west coast of the United States.

TABLE 2.13 LOGISTICS COSTS AS % OF CARGO VALUE

Mode	Commodity	Land distance (km)	Percent cargo value
High value, short life			
Truck	Cotton garments	280	8
Truck	Agricultural produce	1,194	18
Truck	Freight, all kinds	1,615	4
Truck	Yarn	359	3
Medium value			
Truck	Tea	1,380	12
Truck	Wool	1,215	8
Truck	Polypropylene	820	25
Truck	Carpet	1,026	3
Low value			
Truck	Limestone	786	119
Rail	Cement	1,535	44

Source: Logistics cost study, World Bank.

3

Route Selection: Applying a Logistics Viewpoint

The choice of routes for trade flows is made based on four factors: the total logistics costs, time required for door-to-door movement, reliability of delivery, and condition of the delivered goods.[1] Chapter 2 analyzed components of the logistics chain for major trades and routes currently in use in order to explain their impacts on cost and time. This chapter will expand the analysis by comparing the time and costs for these existing routes with those of alternative routes that are not currently in operation, either because of protocol restrictions or infrastructure gaps. The comparative analysis demonstrates how the components of the logistics chain contribute to the competitive advantages of one route over another. The analysis provides a framework for evaluating proposed improvements in a specific route. The impact of these improvements depends on the change in logistics time and cost, as well as the potential for cargo damage, for the route relative to competing alternatives. Similarly, comparative analysis provides a basis for identifying and evaluating new routes by considering their advantage in terms of time, cost, or condition relative to currently used routes. The Bank study team, in collaboration with private sector stakeholders from the subregion, developed the logistics cost model used for the comparative analysis (see Map 6 at the end of this report).

The framework provides a tractable and easy-to-use tool for stakeholders that will help in two types of decisionmaking: (a) to determine which of the routes available is less inefficient and (b) to determine which of the components of the transport logistics chain on a particular route are problematic, where improvements in the

1. The exports and imports analyzed in Chapter 2 are sold either cost-insurance freight (cif) or ex-factory/farm gate. The imports of polypropylene and wool are bought on a cif basis. The intraregional shipments are sold either cif or ex factory/farm gate. In all cases, the responsibility for the logistics rests with either the shipper or the consignee, not both. Therefore the selection of a route will be based on the complete logistics time and cost. The alternative would be to sell exports at the port on a free on board (fob) basis and to purchase imports cif at the port. When the logistics stop at the port, the selection of a route is decided by both the shipper and the consignee.

short term can bring significant returns in terms of efficiency improvements. Shippers and consignees can use this analytic framework to select routes. Governments and other stakeholders can use it to evaluate policies and investments intended to improve performance on one or more routes.

The objective here is not to recommend any one particular route over others or to suggest that any one of the routes analyzed here is the most efficient. The routes analyzed all have inefficiencies, some more than others. Rather, the focus is on trying to encourage further probing and informed dialogue among stakeholders on the routes where efficiency gains can be achieved in the short term, and where more long-term interventions would be required. The focus is on the information that stakeholders have available when selecting routes for shipping cargo. The objective is to identify those improvements in infrastructure, services, and trade facilitation that allow shippers to offer their goods to selected markets at a lower delivered cost with a delivery time and reliability that is acceptable to that market.

It is important that shippers have options. The choice of route will vary with the type of commodity being shipped and the market for that commodity. Reductions in cost, time, and damage on one route will cause some of the cargo to be diverted from alternative routes. These diversions are not instantaneous, but they can occur rapidly if cargoes are traded in competitive markets. Lower logistics costs allow shippers to compete on delivered price. Faster travel times allow shippers to compete for markets that require shorter delivery times. Less damage allows shippers to compete where the quality of the product is a major concern or where restocking times are long. The following analysis suggests that relatively small changes in the logistics chain can have a big impact on route selection.

This same technique can be used to assess future requirements for logistics services. Already, liberalization of trade and the restructuring of international and domestic transport industries have raised expectations regarding the quality of logistics. Future changes in trade and the transport network will raise not only expectations but also requirements for new routes with lower logistics cost and time, and with greater reliability. These trends are discussed briefly at the end of the chapter. They are important to anticipate since the logistics industry in the region has largely been in a catch-up mode and has acted as a constraint rather than as a catalyst for growth in trade and economic development.

The planned improvements in the regional transport network will raise expectations and lead to a diversion of freight movements to the more efficient routes. The end of this chapter discusses the impact of these improvements on route selection. The type of commodities being shipped are expected to change from predominantly raw and semiprocessed materials to semifinished and finished manufactured goods. The trend toward the production of high-value goods must be complemented by better logistics if producers are to compete in international markets.

A more precise indicator of logistics performance is the variance, rather than the average value, of the times and costs of transportation. It is difficult to obtain data on this variable. This chapter also includes a brief discussion of the impact of variance on the costs to the user. It then looks at the relative importance of the condition of the cargo following shipment and the impact of losses and damage on route choice. Losses and damage not only increase the delivered cost but also add to reorder time and increase inventory cost to cover potential shortfalls in the delivery of acceptable goods. The number of intermediate transfers is important for cargoes that are susceptible to loss of damage. The form of shipment is important because it affects both time and damage. Containers and bulk cargoes can be moved more quickly with less damage if handled with appropriate equipment. Several of the selected routes involved container movements, but part of the transport was in break bulk because of physical or regulatory constraints. Bulk cargo is often bagged at a port or transfer point between rail and truck transport, thereby increasing losses and delivery times.

This chapter begins with a comparative analysis of five of the routes that the previous chapter discussed. The analysis is based on current charges and performance. Comparisons are made with alternative routes that have been suggested by users and other stakeholders, or are in the process of being made available because of ongoing bilateral or multilateral negotiations, upgrades to the physical infrastructure, or both factors. These alternatives have specific advantages that may or may not be significant when placed in the context of the total costs for movement of the cargo. Using the same contest, the chapter reviews various proposals for improving the efficiency of the logistics for the existing and proposed routes. Based on the result, a series of initiatives are proposed for improving the selection of routes available by building on the recommendations of the previous chapter.

COMMODITIES, MODES, AND ROUTES: SELECTED CASE STUDIES

The five cargo flows selected for comparative analysis were presented in the previous chapter. Three are extraregional trade in carpets, tea, and general cargo (or FAK), and two are intraregional trades in cement and fruits. The comparisons also consider routes through other countries, especially Bangladesh and India, which are shorter and may offer potential savings in cost and time

for the landlocked regions of Nepal, Bhutan, and Northeastern India.

Case 1: Exporting High-Value Goods from a Landlocked Country to an International Market

Carpet is exported from Nepal to European markets via Calcutta port. The carpets are containerized at Birganj, which is 165 kilometers from Kathmandu. The container trucks are cleared by Nepalese customs and, after an overnight wait at the Nepal-India border, enter Raxaul for clearance on the Indian side. The entire trip by road from Kathmandu to Calcutta port, plus the time in port, averages eight days. This includes a two-day wait to enter the port. It takes an additional four days for clearing customs and loading the cargo on the vessel. The cargo is then shipped east to Singapore for transshipment to a larger ocean vessel heading west to Europe.

The freight forwarders in Nepal are proposing the use of the port at Nhava Sheva (Jawaharlal Nehru Port Trust, or JNPT) on the western coast of India as an alternative to Calcutta once the Bhairawa ICD becomes operational (Map 8 at the end of this report).[2] This would allow direct shipments to Europe instead of feeding through Singapore. The new route would be by truck from Kathmandu through Bhairawa to Nautanwa, India, where the cargo would be packed into containers. The containers would be transported to the ICD at Moradabad and placed on rail cars for shipment to Mumbai and the JNPT container terminal. Although the land transport distance is three to four times as far as the distance to Calcutta port, the ocean portion offers considerable savings in freight rates and shipping times.

---

2. Nepalese cargo has access through the ports at Kandla and Nhava Sheva on the western coast of India in addition to Calcutta port.

by road

TABLE 3.1   CASE 1—HIGH-VALUE EXPORTS FROM A LANDLOCKED COUNTRY TO EUROPE

CONSIGNMENT ATTRIBUTES

Commodity type	Carpet
Shipment size	1 TEU
Origin	Kathmandu, Nepal
Destination	Munich, Germany
Via	Bremen Port, Germany
Shipment value	$90,000

	ROUTE 3-1 ATTRIBUTES Kathmandu-Birgunj/ Raxaul-Calcutta Port-Bremen		ROUTE 3-2 ATTRIBUTES Kathmandu-Bhairawa-Nautanwa- Moradabad-Mumbai (JNPT)-Bremen	
	Cost (US$)	Time (hours)	Cost (US$)	Time (hours)
Transport & handling				
Inland transport	480.00	117	740.00	88
Cargo handling	260.00	74	463.00	155
Ocean freight	1,200.00	528	750.00	336
Cross-border processing				
Cargo transfer	261.00	164 *waiting to enter port*	125.00	37
Customs inspection	405.00	20	202.33	7
Trade-related logistics				
Time cost of goods	1,252.45		864.09	
Insurance or pilferage & damage	675.00		675.00	
Documentation & forwarding	450.00		450.00	
Bank processing for letter of credit	360.00		360.00	

KEY RESULTS		
Transport logistics cost (US$)	5,343	4,629
Transport logistics time (hours)	903	623

Source: Logistics cost study, World Bank.

It has the additional advantage of better productivity and fewer delays at Nhava Sheva than at Calcutta port. Table 3.1 shows the cost and time comparison of the two routes.

Although there is about a 14 percent reduction in cost for the route via the JNPT, the more substantial benefit is a 30 percent reduction in travel time from nearly 38 days to 26 days. The land route to the JNPT is more costly because of the longer distance, but the travel time is reduced by more than one day because of the higher speed on the rail connection between Moradabad and the JNPT. The three-day time for transferring cargo from truck to rail at the Moradabad ICD and 1.5 days in Nhava Sheva port is comparable to the six days spent at Calcutta port. The reduction in ocean transport time is substantial because the route from Calcutta is assumed to include a three-day voyage to Singapore and a five-day wait at Singapore for connection to the mother ship. The JNPT route time could be reduced by one day through tighter coordination in the packing of containers and loading on the rail cars. Further efficiencies could be obtained if the transshipment from road to rail could be avoided altogether at Moradabad. With the operationalization of the rail ICD at Birganj, it would be feasible to ship containerized carpets all the way by rail from Birganj across India to the JNPT.

Although the new route through Nhava Sheva offers substantial savings in time and cost for cargoes shipped to Europe, the same does not apply for shipments to Asia. The latter would require shipping the cargo from Nhava Sheva back through Singapore. Surprisingly, the difference in costs and time with this doubling back would not be that much greater than the route through Calcutta.

Carpets are high-value commodities, and shippers are interested in minimizing the number of handlings. This is better accomplished by shipping containers through Nhava Sheva. Although carpets do not have short order times, they do have a high carrying cost so that a one-month reduction in delivery time will produce a saving to the shipper of about $1000 per container shipment. More importantly, the faster route allows Nepal to compete in markets that require tighter logistics and shorter order times.

This case also suggests that efficient train operations can play a role in the movement of high-value cargoes over long distances. More importantly, it shows that inefficient ports can have a major impact on route selection. Even if the time in Calcutta could be reduced to four days and the cross-border movement could be reduced to one day (especially once the Birganj ICD is operational), the route through the JNPT would still be nine days shorter for shipments to Europe.

Case 2: Exporting Medium-Value Goods From a Landlocked Region To a Third Country

The second case concerns tea shipped from Assam to Europe. Tea produced in Assam is exported to foreign markets through an all-India route, either by rail from an ICD at Gauhati to Haldia port or by road from Assam to Calcutta port. Let us consider the latter case. The tea is crated at the exporter's premise and trucked to Calcutta port. The 1,380-kilometer trip via Shiliguri requires about seven days. In Calcutta, the cargo is checked by customs and loaded into containers at the port's container freight station. It is drayed to the container terminal and subsequently loaded onto an oceangoing vessel. The total processing time on average is 6.75 days. The ocean route involves transshipment via Colombo or Singapore before continuing on to Europe, taking a total of 23.5 days. The major avoidable delays occur at the port of Calcutta.

An alternative route for Assamese tea exports could be through Bangladesh via the port of Chittagong. This route is not one that is in use because of the absence of a bilateral agreement between Bangladesh and India providing transit access to cargo from Northeastern India. If the two countries were to come to an agreement on this issue, then a possible routing could be from Assam south to Agartala (Tripura), crossing over to Bangladesh at Akhaura and on to Chittagong—

TABLE 3.2   CASE 2—MEDIUM-VALUE EXPORTS FROM A LANDLOCKED REGION TO EUROPE

CONSIGNMENT ATTRIBUTES

Commodity type	Tea
Shipment size	8.4 tons
Origin	Karimganj
Destination	Liverpool, United Kingdom
Via	Liverpool, United Kingdom
Shipment value	$20,000

	ROUTE 3-5 ATTRIBUTES Karimganj-Gauhati-Siliguri-Raiganj-Calcutta		ROUTE 3-6 ATTRIBUTES Karimganj-Agartala-Chittagong-Liverpool, United Kingdom	
	Cost (US$)	Time (hours)	Cost (US$)	Time (hours)
Transport & handling				
Inland transport	620.00	168	117.00	29
Cargo handling	205.00	16	328.00	37
Ocean freight	1,250.00	564	1,250.00	585
Cross-border processing				
Cargo transfer	265.00	150	78.00	177
Customs inspection	120.00	12	100.00	39
Trade-related logistics				
Time cost of goods	280.48		267.23	
Insurance or pilferage & damage	200.00		200.00	
Documentation & forwarding	100.00		100.00	
Bank processing for letter of credit	80.00		80.00	

KEY RESULTS		
Transport logistics cost (US$)	3,120	2,520
Transport logistics time (hours)	910	867

Source: Logistics cost study, World Bank.

a distance of about 530 kilometers (Map 9 at the end of this report). If the current policy of prohibiting foreign vehicles into Bangladesh continues, this would mean that the cargo is transferred to Bangladeshi trucks from Indian trucks at the border. Assuming that there is no congestion, the processing time at the border would be about 19 hours and cost US$72, or $8.60 per ton. At Chittagong, it would require an average of nine days for the cargo to clear customs, be loaded into a container, and wait to be loaded onto a vessel. The ocean voyage from Chittagong to Europe is similar to that from Calcutta (via Singapore). This route would save about 19 percent in total cost, as Table 3.2 shows, but the savings in time is insignificant because of the dominance of the ocean movement. The shorter road route (by over 60 percent) would save about 5.5 days, but the time for cargo transfer and customs clearance at the border would add about 3 days. Because Chittagong has less efficient handling, the time the cargo spends in port is about 2.5 days longer. Overall, the shorter route through Chittagong port produces transport time savings of less than 2 days.

The potential advantage of a shorter route through Chittagong is compromised by delays at the border and the requirement to transfer cargo to Bangladeshi trucks. Since the cargo is not containerized, the contents are sensitive to damage, even though tea exporters limit the potential for damage by packing tea in relatively sturdy crates. The choice of route is also affected by the delays at port, which in turn are a function of port performance and frequency in sailings. It is likely that a choice would be made based on the availability of sailings to Europe. The delays on both routes could be significantly reduced with improved port performance. The time in Calcutta could be reduced to four to five days, while the time in Chittagong for packing and waiting for the vessel could be reduced by two to three days. With these improvements the route through Chittagong would be faster and less costly, and the delivery time would be reduced to about 40 days.

Additional time savings could be achieved if Indian trucks were allowed to carry the cargo to Chittagong and if the tea could be transported in containers through Bangladesh.[3] The elimination of the transshipment requirement at the India-Bangladesh border would provide savings in time and cost, but more importantly would reduce the cargo damage. This alone would lower the logistics cost by about 0.25 percent of the value of the cargo.

With the changes in the long-term road and rail transport network envisioned in the subregion, (or even with the current networks), it would be possible to send tea containerized all the way to JNPT if the choice of land routes were expanded to include the rail connection to Nhava Sheva. Initial estimates indicate reduced travel time of an additional 1 to 1.5 weeks and reduced shipping costs of about US$200 compared with the Chittagong route.

Case 3: Intraregional Movement of Break-Bulk Cargo of Essential Commodities to a Landlocked Region

Northeast India obtains most of its essential commodities from the rest of India. The third case examines the transportation of general cargo (freight of all kinds or FAK) from the warehouses in Calcutta to Agartala, Tripura (Table 3.3). The goods are carried on trucks in break-bulk form from Calcutta, the closest major market supplying these goods, through Shiliguri to Agartala in Tripura. The 1,615-kilometer journey from warehouse to Tripura requires about eight days. Because this is a direct movement, there are no international border crossings and no delays for customs clearances or handling cargo along the way.[4]

There have been recent debates in Bangladesh on possible options for providing Indian cargo

---

3. Container movement on road within Bangladesh is nonexistent. The main mode for moving containerizable goods in the Dhaka-Chittagong corridor is by rail, which also is underutilized. See Background Note 4.

4. Constraints in state border crossings within India are not included here.

TABLE 3.3   CASE 3—MEDIUM-VALUE EXPORTS WITHIN THE REGION

CONSIGNMENT ATTRIBUTES	
Commodity type	FAK
Shipment size	8 tons
Origin	Calcutta
Destination	Agartala
Shipment value	$24,000

| | Calcutta-Raiganj-Siliguri-Gauhati-Karimganj-Agartala | | Calcutta-Petrapole-Benapole-Daulatdia Ghat-Aricha Ferry-Narayanganj-Bhairab Ferry-Brahmanbaria-Ashuganj-Akhoura-Agartala | | | | | |
| | All India | | Proposed transshipment through Bangladesh | | Reduced delays through Bangladesh | | Without transshipment | |
	Cost (US$)	Time (hours)	Cost (US$)	Time (hours)	Cost (US$)	Time (hours)	Cost (US$)	Time (hours)
Transport & handling								
Inland transport	760	180	263	41	263	41	263	41
Cargo handling	278	18	270	20	270	20	270	20
Ocean freight	—	—	—	—	—	—	—	—
Cross-border processing								
Cargo transfer	—	—	106	35	106	35	0	0
Customs inspection	—	—	125	151.5	125	55.5	75	12
Trade-related logistics								
Time cost of goods	73		96		83		96	
Insurance or pilferage & damage	240		180		180		180	
Documentation & forwarding	60		240		240		240	
Bank processing for letter of credit	96		96		96		96	

KEY RESULTS				
Transport logistics cost (US$)	1,507	1,376	1,363	1,220
Transport logistics time (hours)	198	247.5	151.5	73

Source: Logistics cost study, World Bank.

transshipments access through Bangladesh. An alternative routing would be for the cargo destined to the Northeastern Indian states to be routed through Bangladesh, thereby reducing the land route by 1,000 kilometers. A possible routing for the cargo could be via the Petrapole (India)-Benapole (Bangladesh) border crossing on the western side and enter Northeastern India at the Akhoura (Bangladesh)-Agartala (India) crossing (Map 10 at the end of this report). The route would include ferry crossings at Aricha and Bhairab.

With the current policies of not allowing foreign trucks into Bangladesh, this would require transfer of cargo at the Petrapole-Benapole border crossing to Bangladeshi trucks on the western side and again at the Akhoura- Agartala border crossing to Indian trucks. The route could reduce trucking time by about six days, but the cross-border procedures and transshipment of cargo at both sets of border crossings (Petrapole-Benapole and Akhoura-Agartala) add back eight days. The savings in trucking costs (over 50 percent) would be offset by the increased costs for cargo inspection, transshipment, and document processing at the two border crossings. There would also be the potential for additional damage during the transfer of cargo from Indian trucks to Bangladeshi trucks and back to Indian trucks. In this situation, the shorter route through Bangladesh is not significantly different in cost (less than 10 percent cost savings) and, in fact, requires 50 hours more logistics time, as shown in Table 3.3 (column 2). The routing through Bangladesh with transshipment would reduce the line-haul transport time by over 75 percent, but there would be a significant increase in the total logistics time due to the border crossing problems. Taking average estimates provided by private sector members in the subregion, the biggest problems are at the Benapole–Petrapole border crossing. They include two days of waiting in line at the border, and over 2.5 days for cross-border clearance at customs. Furthermore, there

would be customs clearance at Akhoura and at Agartala (over two days) and transshipment requirements at both sides. It must be emphasized that these are average estimates that do not include strikes and other incidents that are common to the subregion, which can increase delays by 60 to 100 percent.

If the delays for waiting in line at the Petrapole-Benapole border crossing were eliminated, and the procedures at both sets of border crossings between Bangladesh and India were simplified, the time for the transit route could be reduced by four days. This would make the route two days shorter than the route through Siliguri, but there would not be a significant reduction in cost. (Table 3.3, column 3).

A scenario to consider would be along the lines of practices in other parts of the world, including Europe and developing countries in Central Asia. It would allow Indian trucks transit access to a dedicated corridor across Bangladesh. In this case, there would be no transshipment between Indian and Bangladesh trucks at the borders. If the cargo was allowed to move in-bond in Indian trucks across Bangladesh, an additional 3.25 days would be saved because the trucks could move quickly through customs. The provision for in-bond movement would reduce both cargo transfer costs and the costs for clearance so that the logistics costs would be 19 percent less than the route through Siliguri. The savings in time would be five days (Table 3.3, column 4).

This case demonstrates the importance of border crossings as a source of delay. More efficient border crossings and protocols could produce a dramatic increase in transit traffic. Although the transit through Benapole introduces extreme delays, all cross-border movements are delayed at least one day per border crossing. Efficient in-bond clearance procedures will significantly reduce trip times.

Case 4: Intraregional Movement of Low-Value Commodities to Northeast India

Cement is an important commodity that is transported from Eastern India to Northeastern India. Consider the movement of cement from West Bengal to Agartala in Tripura. It is moved in bags on broad-gauge rail from Calcutta through Gauhati and Lumding and then down to Karimganj and Agartala. This is a total distance of 1,635 kilometers with no border crossings, assuming that the supplier and the customer have direct access to the rail sidings (Map 11 at the end of this report). The trip takes 2.5 days and costs about US$26 per ton (Table 3.4).

The alternative would be to move the cement through Bangladesh by rail, a route that is not currently in use due to the lack of agreement between the two countries. The current broad-gauge rail connection from India extends into Bangladesh (at Darshana-Gede and Petrapole-Benapole) and stretches across the Jamuna bridge as a dual-gauge line. The broad-gauge link is being extended to Joydepur and Tongi (Background Note 3). A meter-gauge link connects Tongi to Akhoura. There are tentative plans to link the broad-gauge rail between Akhoura, Bangladesh, and Agartala, India, on the eastern side of Bangladesh's border with India. If we assume that the two countries agree on protocol to allow cargo movement for the Northeastern Indian states by rail via Bangladesh, this route would require one shift from broad gauge to meter gauge at Tongi and then back to broad at Akhoura (assuming that the other broad-gauge links are in place and completed as planned).

This alternative route would reduce the total distance by more than 1,010 kilometers, but it would require an exchange of locomotives at both borders. If this exchange is efficient, the route has a competitive advantage in time and cost. The line-haul time would be shorter by 1.25 days. The

transshipment and customs clearance was assumed to add a half-day, but this could easily increase to four to five days with a missed connection between Indian and Bangladeshi trains.

The cost for rail transport would be 43 percent less on the alternative route, while the handling and clearance would add back only 2 percent. There could be additional offsets related to delays and damage. This route would require additional handling—and handling of bagged cement inevitably involves significant losses. Missed connections at the border and losses during the transfer from broad to narrow gauge could create shortfalls in deliveries. On balance this route would be considerably less costly due to savings from the considerably shorter line-haul distance. However, this assumes that gauge conversions are completed, particularly the Akhoura-Agartala link that is still at a preliminary stage of planning. If not, the portion of meter gauge requiring a transshipment, either between rail cars or to and from trucks, would substantially increase the handling costs and the damage to the cargo.

An inland water route from Calcutta to Ashuganj by inland waterways transport was also considered. This route is available for transiting through Bangladesh to and from the Northeastern Indian states because of a bilateral protocol that was revised in October 1999. The route would require trucking the cargo from the cement plant to Calcutta, loading it on the barges, and shipping it to Ashuganj, where the cement would be loaded on trucks for delivery.

This route adds 10 days to the line-haul time and several days for loading and unloading the barges (Table 3.4, column 3). The result is a nine-fold increase in logistics time compared to the railway transit route. Furthermore, the logistics costs would increase by about 23 percent, not counting the substantial increase in cargo loss

TABLE 3.4   CASE 4—INTRAREGIONAL MOVEMENT OF LOW-VALUE, BULK COMMODITIES TO LANDLOCKED REGION

CONSIGNMENT ATTRIBUTES

Commodity type	Cement
Shipment size	2,200 tons
Origin	Calcutta
Destination	Agartala
Shipment value	$133,000

	ROUTE 3-9 ATTRIBUTES		ROUTE 3-10 ATTRIBUTES		ROUTE 3-11 ATTRIBUTES	
	Calcutta-New Jalpaiguri-Bongaigon-Gauhati-Lumding-Karimganj		Calcutta-Gede-Darsana-Ishurdi-Jaydevpur-Dhaka-Tongi-Akhaura-Agartala		Calcutta-Narayanganj-Ashuganj by barge and Ashuganj-Agartala by truck	
	Cost (US$)	Time (hours)	Cost (US$)	Time (hours)	Cost (US$)	Time (hours)
Transport & handling						
Inland transport	58,400	48	33,468	18	4,300	3
Cargo handling	1,022	12	2,237	24	9,774	108
Inland waterway transport & handling	—	—	—	—	29,314	264
Cross border processing						
Cargo transfer	—	—	—	—	511	48
Customs inspection	—	—	400	17	300	120
Trade-related logistics						
Time cost of goods	123		121		1,113	
Insurance or pilferage & damage	1,330		998		1,330	
Documentation & forwarding	665		665		333	
Bank processing for letter of credit	532		532		532	
KEY RESULTS						
Transport logistics cost (US$)	62,072		38,421		47,507	
Transport logistics time (hours)	60		59		543	

Source: Logistics cost study, World Bank.

during the transfer between trucks and barges. However, the inland waterways transport route remains preferable to the route through Siliguri in terms of logistics costs—it is 23 percent less by inland waterways transport than by the long all-India rail route around India's so-called chicken's neck. The disadvantage in logistics time could also be reduced through the introduction of navigation aids, including those for night navigation.

Case 5: Movement of Perishable Commodities from Nepal: 8.5 Tons of Apples from Kathmandu to Dhaka

The final case analyzes the movement of apples from Kathmandu to Dhaka (see Background Note 7 for a full report). For both Bhutan and Nepal, the most important trade goods with the region are vegetables, fruits, and related produce. The analysis does not concern alternative routes but rather the importance of simplified border crossing procedures. The recent Phulbari corridor agreement among Bangladesh, India, and Nepal allows Nepalese goods, particularly agricultural produce such as jhumla apples, to find a market in Bangladesh. The apples travel from Nepal to Dhaka as loose cargo on trucks. The initial movement is to the border with India in a Nepalese truck, a distance of 619 kilometers. The truck crosses Nepal at Kakarvitta and travels through Panitanki and Phulbari in India to enter Bangladesh at Banglabandh, a distance of 43 kilometers (Map 12 at the end of this report).

The Nepalese consignment is escorted by Indian police over this route. When it crosses over to Bangladesh, the cargo is transferred to Bangladeshi trucks and carried 532 kilometers to Dhaka. The Banglabandh border crossing is a fledgling one, and it does not have a formal customs office or an official in place. The nearest customs office is in Panchagarh, about 58 kilometers away. It has to be informed every time a Nepalese consignment is expected to arrive. Total

trucking time is about three days. Another 1.75 days is spent in crossing the borders and transferring cargo between trucks. The time and cost of transferring the cargo between trucks is a relatively small part of the total logistics time and cost, but this does not include the damage to the apples as a result of the transfer. Also, the impediments faced in the process of clearing four customs points (at the two border crossings) and the absence of a customs office at Banglabandh do not provide positive incentives for trade.

The inefficiencies could be reduced if Nepalese trucks were permitted to carry the cargo all of the way to Dhaka. The impact in terms of travel time and direct costs would be relatively small, but the reduction in damage could be significant. A reduction in losses of 1 percent of the cargo value would be equivalent to the savings from handling costs and produce a total savings of 10 percent. A similar kind of analysis could be done for Bhutan, which also supplies perishables such as fruit and fruit-based products to Bangladeshi markets. These commodities are transported from Phuntsholing, Bhutan, through Jaigon and Changrabandh in India. They enter Bangladesh at Burimari, where they are transferred to Bangladeshi trucks to be carried to Dhaka markets. For sustained and improved regional markets for agricultural and horticultural products from Nepal and Bhutan, improved logistics would be key to reducing damage.

HIGHLIGHTS OF CASE STUDIES

The accuracy of the comparative analysis is limited because performance on existing routes is being compared with expected performance on new routes that are not in operation, either because of the absence of bilateral protocols and agreements or because of infrastructure inadequacies. However, these examples clearly demonstrate the importance of being able to select among alternative routes. A fixed number of border crossings may be appropriate because the resources required to operate these crossings are limited, but there is little justification for limiting the routes between these crossings.[5] The freedom to choose alternative routes can also help to reduce congestion at the major crossings. See Table 2.6 for a list of current and alternative routes.

Route selection is affected by the bottlenecks at the border crossings and seaports as well as by the condition of the links. The reaction of shippers to the growing congestion at the Benapole crossing is a case in point. The situation deteriorated to the point that shippers rerouted through remote and unmanned border crossings rather than wait for days at the border, especially if they were carrying perishable cargo. This issue is now being resolved through an expansion of the border crossing (discussed in the previous chapter).

Based on the comparative analysis, the following route-specific observations can be made:

- Intraregional shipments of fruits, vegetables, and other perishables from Bhutan and Nepal to India and Bangladesh require much better logistics. This can be achieved by allowing the cargo to move in a single truck from origin to destination and by ensuring that clearance time at the border on both sides does not exceed six hours.

- High-value exports from Nepal to the Pacific Rim require faster handling at Calcutta, Chittagong, and Haldia, while shipments to Europe and the U.S. East Coast require direct (intermodal) connections to the JNPT. Both

require containerization of the cargoes at the earliest point in the logistics chain. The ability to ship in containers will be substantially improved with the operationalization of the three ICDs on the Nepalese border.

- Truck routes via Bangladesh can offer reductions in time and cost for medium-value goods moving between East and Northeast India. This will require an effective protocol for in-bond movements and coordination between customs checkpoints to significantly reduce delays and eliminate transshipment. The savings to the shippers should be sufficient to support tolls to cover the cost for road maintenance resulting from the increase in transit traffic.

- For trade in high-value goods between India and Bangladesh, trucks will be the dominant, if not exclusive, mode. Travel time will be the major concern and route selection will be based on reducing door-to-door delivery time. Significant improvements in rail operations will be needed if this mode is to capture some of this traffic.

- Low-value goods, especially bulk cargoes, will move primarily by rail because of the higher costs for trucking and the longer transit times for inland water. However, inland waterways could play a more prominent role in the transport of the low-value bulk cargoes that move between Calcutta and north and east Bangladesh, which is not yet served by broad-gauge rail. With improvements in night navigation aids, the transit times by inland waterways could be reduced.

- If the Indian and Bangladesh railways continue to integrate their systems and to extend their broad-gauge networks, they might capture some medium-value break-bulk cargoes. However, delays will continue at the border

---

5. There are many reasons for restricting the use of routes by international traffic, including issues of security and safety.

unless compatible rolling stock is introduced and the shortage of locomotives ends.

- Seaports are very important factors in determining route selection because of the large delays and high costs for transferring cargo through the port. More cargo would be routed through efficient seaports that eliminate unnecessary customs procedures and delays in cargo handling.

DAMAGES, DELAYS, AND CORRUPTION

In this and previous chapters, frequent references have been made of the cost of damages; however, data were not available to determine how damage varied by route. The insurance for pilferage and damage was assumed to be 1 percent of cargo value for longer routes and 0.75 percent for shorter routes. Insurance covers only part of the losses because the existing legislation regarding carriage of goods does not clearly assign liabilities.

In order to understand the impact of damages, comparisons were made between the reported logistics costs and typical costs for damages. It was assumed that the losses per intermediate transfer average between 0.25 and 1.5 percent of cargo value, depending on the type of commodity and cargo form. The lower rate applies to containerized cargo and the higher rate to agricultural products shipped in break-bulk form. Table 3.5 shows the number of intermediate handlings and expected losses per handling.

TABLE 3.5   ESTIMATED IMPACT OF DAMAGE

Origin/destination	Mode	Cargo	Total time (days)	No. of handlings	Damage per intermediate handling (percent)
Domestic					
Calcutta-Argatala	Rail	Cement	9.8	2	1.00
Calcutta-Argatala	Truck	General cargo	8.3	3	0.50
Regional					
Kathmandu-Dhaka	Truck	Agricultural produce	4.6	3	1.50
Thimpu-Dhaka	Truck	Limestone	3.6	3	0.75
Calcutta-Dhaka	Truck	Yarn	11.3	3	0.50
Calcutta-Argatala	Barge	Cement	19.0	4	0.75
International					
Karimganj-Calcutta-Liverpool	Truck	Tea	37.4	3	0.25
New Zealand-Calcutta-Kathmandu	Truck	Wool	33.4	4	0.50
Singapore-Calcutta-Thimpu	Truck	Polypropylene	29.5	4	0.50
Dhaka-Chittagong-United States	Truck	Cotton garments	34.3	3	0.25
Kathmandu-Calcutta-Bremen	Truck/rail	Carpet	39.1	4	0.25

Source: Logistics cost study estimates, World Bank.

TABLE 3.6 IMPACT OF DAMAGE AND DELAYS

Origin/destination	Cargo	Logistic cost (as percentage of cargo value)	Delay cost[a] (as percentage of cargo value)	Damage[b] (as percentage of cargo value)
Domestic				
Calcutta-Argatala	Cement	44.7	0.39	1.00
Calcutta-Argatala	General cargo	4.3	0.17	0.50
Regional				
Kathmandu-Dhaka	Agricultural produce	18.1	0.59	1.50
Thimpu-Dhaka	Limestone	119.3	0.11	0.75
Calcutta-Dhaka	Yarn	3.2	0.45	0.50
Calcutta-Argatala	Cement	58.7	0.76	1.50
International				
Karimganj-Calcutta-Liverpool	Tea	12.3	2.25	0.25
New Zealand-Calcutta-Kathmandu	Wool	8.0	0.67	1.00
Singapore-Calcutta-Thimpu	Polypropylene	24.6	0.59	1.00
Dhaka-Chittagong-United States	Cotton garments	4.1	0.69	0.25
Kathmandu-Calcutta-Bremen	Carpets	2.9	0.78	0.50

a. Additional cost for the consignee's inventory, assuming delay equal to 15 % of total travel time.
b. Excludes initial loading and final unloading.
Source: Logistics cost study estimates, World Bank.

The costs of delays to the shipper were included in the logistics costs presented above, and they are based on the estimated carrying costs to the shipper for the value of cargo while in transit. This assumes that the shipper borrows against the letter of credit for the time the cargo is shipped to when it is received. The other cost of delay derives from the uncertainty of the period of shipment. The consignee must maintain sufficient inventory to prevent an outage if goods are not delivered in the maximum delivery time.[6] The cost of financing this inventory is the value of the in-cremental inventory required, multiplied by the annual rate of interest paid by the consignee.[7] This additional inventory is then related to the annual shipment of goods to obtain a percentage of cargo value. For the purposes of comparison, the reorder rate was assumed to be 3 months for textiles and carpets, 1.5 months for building materials, 1 month for tea, and 2 weeks for agricultural products. Table 3.6 summarizes the results, which assume the delays are 15 percent of the expected transit time, including ocean transport.

6. If the product is reordered every x weeks and maximum delivery time is y weeks greater than the average, then the minimum stock at the time of order must be the amount consumed during the average delivery time plus y weeks.

The net impact of the uncertainty in delivery time is that the consignee must maintain an extra y weeks worth of inventory or x/y of a typical shipment.

7. The prevailing commercial interest rate is used. The proper rate, the consignee's cost of capital, is larger.

Table 3.6 compares the costs of delay with damage and logistics costs. The impact of damage and delay are greatest for the high-value cargoes because the amounts are comparable to the other logistics costs. For Nepalese carpets, Bangladeshi garments, Indian yarn, and imported wool, the costs for damage and delay is equal to 25 to 45 percent of the logistics costs. For Bhutanese limestone and Indian cement, these costs are equal to just 1 to 3 percent of the logistics costs. For Indian FAK, Nepalese agricultural products, and Assam tea, the costs are 11 to 20 percent of the logistics costs. Assam tea is most sensitive to delay because the logistics time and the reorder time are similar, whereas Bhutanese limestone is the least sensitive because the logistics time is small compared to the reorder time. Damage is more important for the non-containerized cargo with several intermediate handlings. The requirement for introducing containers to reduce damage is greatest for agricultural products. The reduction in intermediate handlings to reduce damage is greatest for cement.

The impact of corruption was also examined by requesting information on informal payments. These include not only payments to customs officials at the border crossings, but also payments to police at checkpoints along the route and to cargo handlers in port. Most of the information collected was anecdotal, although an attempt was made to relate payments to shipments as shown in Table 3.7. These indicate small costs relative to the value of the cargo, with the exception of the imports of polypropylene.

Examples of informal costs cited by shippers include:

- 30 percent of invoice value for a consignment on the Bangladesh-Phulbari corridor through Kakarvitta,

- US$150 per consignment on imports and exports via Haldia,

- Rs6,000 per container and Rs2,000 to Rs3,000 per truck on average at the Indian border crossing points, and

- Rs80 per ton at the Raxaul-Birgunj border crossing, payable at the Indian side of the Nepalese border.

VARIATIONS IN TRANSPORT LOGISTICS PERFORMANCE AND COST

The logistics cost estimates presented earlier are subject to variations as dictated by operating conditions prevalent at the time. Under less favorable operating conditions, processing the activities in the transport chain can take much longer and therefore affect transport logistics costs adversely. As interest in minimizing inventories and shortening reorder times has increased, so has concern for the reliability of shipment time and cost. Each link in a logistics chain poses a risk of additional delay and, when appropriate, additional informal payments. Reducing the uncertainty associated with the cost and time for delivery has already been given greater priority than absolute cost and time for some trades. Unfortunately, information on this variation is difficult to collect. The small sample of stakeholders consulted during the exercise did not allow for a reliable estimate of the variance in logistics time and cost. However, the stakeholders did estimate that about 10 percent of the shipments during the course of the year experience above-average delays. These occur during the following:

- **Claiming shipment at the gateway port.** This can occur because of late notification of ship arrival notice, long preparation time for assembling documents for customs clearance, or other reasons, thereby increasing port clearance time by 14 days.

- **Port terminal processing.** Equipment breakdowns can increase processing time by three days and a labor strike can cause delays of more than a week.

- **Customs clearance at the port.** Any of a number of issues, including incorrect documentation, container inspection necessitated by a broken seal, or uncertainty over the dutiable amount of import item, can increase the clearance time by one day to (in the case of incorrect documentation) more than a week.

- **Egress from and access to the port.** Frequent political strikes and transport industry strikes outside the port cause congestion and inhibit mobility, thereby increasing the transit time by one to several days.

- **Road-line haul between the port and the border crossing or destination.** Delays of one day to more than 15 days can result from truck accidents, truck breakdown, police inspection or harassment, the driver visiting home if it is along the route, truck bans in the city, ferry crossings, and other issues.

- **Land exit or entry port in the transit country.** Congested traffic access and egress (particularly on Mondays in the Nepal-India border), late arrival of sealed cover, and local political strikes may increase the processing time by one to several days.

- **Land entry or exit port in the destination country.** Incorrect or incomplete documentation or disagreement over the description or classification of the goods, as well as the

TABLE 3.7	INFORMAL PAYMENTS	
Route	**Commodity**	**Informal payment** (% *of cargo value*)
Domestic		
Calcutta-Argatala	Cement	0.0–0.3
Calcutta-Argatala	General cargo	0.15–0.5
Regional		
Kathmandu-Dhaka	Agricultural produce	1.2–1.2
Thimpu-Dhaka	Limestone	0.9
Calcutta-Dhaka	Yarn	0.25
Calcutta-Argatala	Cement	0.25
International		
Karimganj-Calcutta-Liverpool	Tea	0.3–.0.5
New Zealand-Calcutta-Kathmandu	Wool	—
Singapore-Calcutta-Thimpu	Polypropylene	1.0–4.3
Dhaka-Chittagong-United States	Cotton garments	0.18
Kathmandu-Calcutta-Bremen	Carpets	0.3

Source: Logistics cost study estimates, World Bank.

valuation of the goods subject to customs duty, may increase the clearance time by two days to more than a week.

The magnitude of the impact of these additional delays depends in many respects on how many delays occur for a given shipment. Conceivably all could occur per shipment in the worst-case situation; alternatively, just one incident could befall a shipment. To demonstrate the high impact on transport logistics cost, calculations for two routes have been made, using data from exporters, freight forwarders, and importers.

The first concerns the case of yarn import from Calcutta to Dhaka. In this case, additional delays are incurred through several points in the system, namely:

- Trucking from Calcutta to Petrapole increased to 24 hours (from 5 hours) because of congested traffic caused by political protests along the way;

- Waiting at Petrapole customs increased to 108 hours (from 84 hours) because of unusually long lines;

- Indian customs clearance at Petrapole increased to 24 hours (from 1 hour), plus speed money (informal payments) doubled, because of incorrect documentation that required fixing at Calcutta;

- Waiting and unloading at the Bangladeshi customs storage area in Benapole increased to 96 hours (from 60 hours) because of equipment breakdown;

- Bangladeshi customs clearance at Benapole increased to 120 hours (from 72 hours), plus speed money doubled, because of incomplete and incorrect documentation that required additional documentation from Dhaka;

- Loading cargo onto Bangladeshi trucks at the Benapole customs storage area increased to 24 hours (from 12 hours) due to equipment breakdown again; and

- Line-haul trucking from Benapole to Dhaka increased to 24 hours (from 12 hours) due to delayed ferry crossing and the untimely arrival at Dhaka during a period when trucks were banned.

The impact of these delays is to increase the cycle time by 64 percent and the transport logistics cost by 9 percent over the results obtained under average conditions.

The second example refers to carpet export from Kathmandu to Bremen. In this case, the additional delays are incurred at the following points in the system:

- Nepalese trucking from Kathmandu to Birgunj customs increased to 24 hours (from 12 hours) due to an accident along the way;

- Unloading and packing cargo into a container in the Birgunj customs storage area increased to 12 hours (from 6 hours) hours due to equipment breakdown;

- Nepalese customs clearance increased to 48 hours (from 3 hours) because of incorrect documentation;

- Loading the container onto an Indian truck increased to 24 hours (from 3 hours) because of a labor strike in the Birgunj customs storage area;

- Trucking to Raxaul at the Indian border increased to 8 hours (from 5 hours) because of traffic congestion between Birgunj and the Indian border;

- Line-haul trucking from Raxaul to Calcutta port increased to 220 hours (from 100 hours) because of a truck breakdown along the way;

- Waiting time to enter Calcutta port increased to 96 hours (from 48 hours) because the truck missed the last sailing and had to wait for the next one;

- Container handling in the terminal increased to 72 hours (from 36 hours) because of labor unrest;

- Waiting for the vessel and loading it increased to 120 hours (from 60 hours) because of equipment breakdown.

The impact of these delays is to increase in the cycle time by 39 percent and the transport logistics cost by 10.7 percent over the results obtained under average conditions.

CONCLUSIONS

The various insights developed in this chapter can be summarized as follows:

- The entire logistics chain must be examined when considering route selection. The information on an individual component can produce incorrect results. For example, relative transport distance is not directly related to either the time or cost of moving cargo along a route. For most of the routes, the procedures at border crossings introduced substantial and avoidable costs and delays that made the route less competitive. Requirements to transfer cargo from one vehicle to another were particularly expensive and time-consuming. Similarly, the seaports were the major source of costs and delays. This could discourage shippers and consignees from choosing a route that relies on a port as a gateway regardless of the route's advantages.

- The problems with customs procedures include not only the annoyance of informal payments but, more importantly, the unnecessary and uncertain delays and the damage that can result during cargo inspections. Some of these delays are due to capacity constraints or lack of cargo-handling equipment rather than inefficient inspection and clearance procedures. Improvements in cross-border procedures could significantly increase the use of a route.

- Certain cargoes have specific problems that affect route selection. For high-value goods with short reorder times, uncertainty with regards to the actual time in transit (measured as a percentage of the average value) introduces a significant cost for importers that they will avoid by seeking the fastest, most reliable route. For cargoes that are susceptible to damage, multiple handlings along a route will be a major disincentive to using a route. Perishable cargoes are susceptible to damage due to intermediate handlings, long travel times, and uncertain delivery times. Shippers of these cargoes will look for reliable services that involve a single vehicle or container. At the extreme are higher-value perishables that will be transported by air freight. Only for the lowest-value, bulk commodities will shippers be concerned exclusively with logistics costs.

- Truck transport normally has a competitive advantage over rail transport, but efficient unit trains can compete effectively for cargo moving over medium to long distances where there are direct rail connections. The short-term improvements in rail transport, such as gauge harmonization, unit train operations, and increased private sector operations, are expected to improve the competitive position of rail transport compared to trucking, especially for containerized cargoes. However, the long-term improvements planned for the road network, such as widening roads and strengthening bridges, will increase the market share of trucking relative to rail.

- Over the next decade typical goods being shipped will increase in value and thereby increase the demand for better logistics. Intraregional trade for Nepal and Bhutan will increasingly be in consumer goods, pharmaceuticals, garments, and fresh fruits and vegetables. All these products will require better logistics, lower costs, and significant reductions in time, if they are to compete in regional markets.

4

Improving Private-Public Partnerships in South Asian Transport and Logistics

This chapter examines the opportunities for public-private partnerships for developing an efficient transportation system in the region. It begins with a review of the views and comments presented in a discussion among private sector transport users and operators in a World Bank-sponsored consultative workshop in Kathmandu on February 4, 1999 (see Background Note 1 for the proceedings). The private sector expressed strong dissatisfaction with the existing state of freight transportation for domestic and international markets, especially the problems of route and mode restrictions, onerous cross-border procedures, and lack of consultation with users in bilateral and multilateral discussions on a cross-country route and mode choices.

Private sector groups are pursuing improvements in trade relations and transport logistics to ensure a smoother flow of goods and cost-effective services among the countries in the region. The purpose of the Kathmandu consultative meeting was to discuss specific regional constraints to the movement of goods and means of facilitating services. Four specific topics were discussed:

- Priority corridors,

- Cost of transit formalities,

- Recommendations for the role of the private sector, and

- Suggestions for government actions

The previous chapter discussed the first two items. The following section covers some of the specific problems identified by the participants. The remaining sections discuss specific examples of private sector involvement and conclude with lessons learned from international experience in private sector involvement in public transport infrastructure.

There was general agreement among the four representative groups about issues affecting regional transit and the need for interaction between the private and public sectors to improve transit of trade in multilateral or bilateral protocols. The Nepal transit facilitation initiative, which included the establishment of a broad-based trade and transport facilitation committee, was seen as a positive step toward bringing together the private and public sectors, providing cost-effective infrastructure, and influencing the renegotiations of transit treaties while prioritizing the facilitation of transit formalities.

The following issues were found to be common to all four countries:

- Poor harmonization of documents and procedures between the countries;

- Cumbersome cross-border procedures due to the high rate of inspections;

- Requirements for multiple copies of numerous types of documents;

- Manual, not automated, processing of documents;

- Regulatory and physical restrictions to potentially cost-effective transit corridors;

- A failure to identify the most cost-effective transit corridors in multilateral and bilateral protocols, partly because of insufficient consultation with the users;

- Customs facilities and communications in need of modernization and streamlining;

- Custom officials in need of more training and export orientation before being posted at borders; and

- Poor dialogue between the public sector in its role of facilitator and the private sector in its roles of user, subject of regulatory systems, and potential contributor to public investment.

Many of these problems could have been avoided if government officials had consulted more closely with business leaders and business people involved in trade and transport before negotiating bilateral agreements and protocols.

The representatives said that these various constraints produced long delays and high costs for transport. The problems they mentioned in specific countries included:

- Gateways in northwestern Bangladesh that link eastern Nepal and Bhutan are limited to Burimari for Bhutanese traffic and Banglabandha for Nepalese traffic.

- Land ports in northwest Bangladesh have poor road access and egress.

- Treaty or protocol agreements established on a bilateral basis between Bangladesh and neighboring countries require double handling of cargo at the border due to the transfer from trucks of one jurisdiction to trucks of another jurisdiction.

- Container transport in Bangladesh is not included in the present transit protocol with India, thereby encouraging costly break-bulk handling of containerizable goods.

- Container escorts are compulsory en route to Calcutta for Nepalese and Bhutanese trade with countries outside the subregion.

- Long lines on both sides of the India-Bangladesh border result from inadequate transshipment facilities, onerous clearance procedures, and lack of truck-to-truck and rail-to-truck transfer facilities.

- Bribery and corruption exist at various official levels at border crossings and ports, which makes the speedy clearance of goods a costly activity.

- Roads are in poor condition in India on the routes to Nepal, Bhutan, and Bangladesh. Particularly bad are sections of roads in Bihar and Uttar Pradesh on routes from Calcutta to Nepal and Bhutan, and heavy congestion on the route from Calcutta to Benapole due to high traffic volume on narrow, poorly maintained two-lane roads.

- Arbitrary procedures exist concerning the exchange of goods between India and Bangladesh, and the prohibition of trucks of one country entering the other.

- Indian railways limit the choice of corridors for cross-border movements of wagons and containers.

- There is a lack of legislation for the transport of containers by road in Bangladesh.

- Transshipments are required from broad- to narrow-gauge railroads in India and Bangladesh.

- Bangladesh railways have capacity constraints, such as short loops and limited rail terminals, which if corrected would improve the utilization of Indian wagon capacity.

- Differences in wagon technology create time delays. This should be addressed in bilateral agreements between India and Bangladesh.

- India and Bangladesh should issue multiple visas to genuine importers and exporters as recommended by the Federation of Indian Chambers of Commerce and Industry (FICCI) and the Federation of Bangladesh Chambers of Commerce and Industry (FBCCI) and their constituent customers.

- The lack of insurance coverage for Indian goods in Bangladeshi government warehouses leads to large losses for Indian exporters.

Bangladeshi insurance companies should provide coverage on import cargo, and banking and insurance norms followed by both nations' banks should be standardized;

- The formats for issuing letter of credit in Bangladeshi banks are not compatible with international informational norms, and nonfulfillment of letter of credit commitments by Bangladeshi banks presents problems for Indian exporters. The FICCI and FBCCI should resolve issues on a case-by-case basis in order to build the confidence of exporters and importers in both countries.

The representatives mentioned problems in specific locations, including:

- Poor performance at Chittagong and Calcutta ports, which increases the cost of trade to and from international markets because of poor management, labor problems, lack of infrastructure, rigid rules and regulations, and the failure of the landlocked cargo owners to claim their shipments in a timely manner. The rail connection between Radhikapur and Birol should be converted from meter gauge to broad gauge.

- The working times at Petrapole and Benapole are not synchronized. That is, operating hours and holidays at the two cross-border points differ, creating inefficiencies in traffic movement.

- Banglabandh has no customs clearance services unless authorities are notified in advance.

- Problems of work duplication at Ranaghat and Gede customs should be resolved by forming an Indian Export Processing Zone in Bangladesh, patterned after the Korean Export Processing Zone.

- Lengthy export procedures at Ranaghat should be reduced by posting an assistant customs commissioner at Ranaghat instead of Krishnanagar, and providing a single window customs clearance at Ranaghat or Gede.

DELEGATES' VIEWS OF THE PRIVATE SECTOR ROLE

The delegations recognized the limitations of the private sector in overcoming infrastructure shortcomings, but they voiced the desire to be consulted through appropriate trade organizations on all decisions concerning the negotiation and ratification of agreements and protocols related to regional trade. They also wanted to be consulted on other regulatory and trade matters. They offered the following comments about their prospective role.

- **Management of landports and logistics facilities.** There is a need for greater private sector involvement in the operation of these facilities and in the development of container transport. The current experience with private sector concessions in the Nepal Multimodal Project was mentioned as a good example of this involvement. Private sector activity should extend to the management of landport facilities and services, cargo-handling facilities and services, container operations, and facilities and labor.

- **Third-party logistics at the landports.** There is a need for the private sector to provide services, including freight forwarding, customs clearance, financial services, storage and warehousing, and general transit and shipping services at seaports and land border crossings. This needs to be supported by appropriate regulatory provisions and adequate government contributions for basic infrastructure facilitation.

- **Operations.** The private sector would work with appropriate government bodies through

its trade associations to pass cost-effective transport policies, such as transit facilitation for Nepalese cargo moving in containers to the JNPT and facilitation of Nepalese and Bhutanese cargo transiting Bangladesh and India.

- **Electronic communications and improved procedures.** The private sector would support the introduction of new customs systems and procedures, especially the electronic communications interface with users. It would contribute to public-private training programs, as are being conducted in Nepal.

EXPECTATIONS ABOUT GOVERNMENT ACTION

Historically, the governments in the region have provided transportation infrastructure and transport services through state-owned corporations (such as the Bangladesh Inland Waterway Transport Corporation, Indian Railways, and Bangladesh Railways). In recent years, the private sector has replaced the government in providing trucking and inland waterway transport, but private sector participation in rail services has been limited. The government continues to provide infrastructure, but this has slowly started to change as government officials accept the need for private financing, especially for ports and expressways.

The delegates made a number of proposals for government action in trade facilitation. These proposals included:

- Harmonize government trade and transport policies and regulations (such as road transport regulations, customs, and insurance and liability) with transit treaty and protocol stipulations to encourage seamless multimodal transport. This includes the compatibility of key procedures and documents for trade, transport, and fiscal transactions. This effort should aim at a "one-stop window."

- Amend transit treaties and protocols to allow for a freer choice of transport routes and service providers, such as carriers and clearing agents. Service providers should operate under the coverage of regionally acceptable document and insurance.

- Institute a program of modernization for customs and cross-border facilities under the joint responsibility of national and local government authorities, supported as necessary by industry and trade associations.

- Increase the use of container transport by removing institutional impediments, such as the protocol between India and Bangladesh, which does not recognize container transport, and Bangladesh's trade and transport legislation, which makes no provision for road transport of containers.

- Construct ICDs in the region to encourage container transport outside of the main India rail transport corridors. This should be the joint concern of government and trade associations, and it should be supported by private investment as appropriate.

- Improve the access to credit and financial intermediation services throughout the region, particularly in the landlocked countries, so carriers can finance the development of an efficient trucking fleet in order to compete in cross-border transport markets.

The public sector should view the private sector not only as a user but also as a potential investor and a facilitator. Legal instruments and bilateral agreements should reflect the public and private sector interaction. Government officials should rely on the support of the private sector trade associations when defining the needs and responsibilities for operation and shared investment.

ORGANIZATIONS FOR INNOVATIVE PRIVATE-PUBLIC INVESTMENTS

Private sector-led activities in the subregion are a nascent but emerging force. There have been several interesting and innovative ways in which private sector participation has been elicited in the various countries. Some of these activities have been in predominantly public sectors. Some initiatives were geared toward the creation of a better investment environment with more active private sector participation. In other cases, the private sector is directly involved in logistic services. Four organizations that have been established to address private sector participation in logistics and transport infrastructure are the Emerging East Initiative, Infrastructure Investment Facilitation Center, Infrastructure Development Company Limited, and West Bengal Infrastructure Development Corporation.

Emerging East Initiative

West Bengal, Bangladesh, Bhutan, Nepal, and East India have joined efforts to coordinate economic development through a multicountry private sector forum under the Emerging East Initiative. This group has identified goals to improve trade and shipments of goods within the region, including the need for standardizing procedures and documents. This endeavor was initiated by the Indian Chamber of Commerce and has the support of the various countries involved as well as that of the Asian Development Bank. The forum is comprised of various industry and business leaders in the different nations as well as chamber members from each region. Its mission statement includes the following:

- To help promote subregional economic cooperation in the Emerging East Region, comprising of Bangladesh, Bhutan, Nepal and Eastern India;

- To accelerate economic development in this region for the mutual benefit of all the countries and its people;

- To identify joint initiatives that would further the cause of subregional co-operation in trade, investment, tourism, infrastructure, services and any other areas that could enhance the growth of the subregion;

- To strengthen the private sector and its organizations in individual nations of this subregion;

- To discuss, negotiate, promote, and undertake continuous dialogue with the government and relevant authorities;

- To promote the objectives of subregional co-operation and implementation of agreed initiatives, such as, those under the South Asian Growth Quadrangle;

- To propagate the benefits of subregional co-operation through the media to enhance the awareness of the people and the decision-makers in this region.

Infrastructure Investment Facilitation Center

Bangladesh has committed itself to improvement through its support of such institutions as the Infrastructure Investment Facilitation Center (IIFC). This is a group that the Bangladeshi government and the World Bank set up to help the government encourage private sector participation. Financing and technical assistance comes in part from the United Kingdom's Department for International Development and the Canadian International Development Agency. The IIFC's resources include expertise in engineering, economics, finance, competition and regulation, procurement, and contracting.

The IIFC is organized into two teams. One, which works on the design phase, is comprised of concession policy and design team specialists; the other, which works on the implementation phase, is comprised of transaction award and execution team specialists. The spectrum of partnership arrangements that are available range from a service contract to management contracts to leases, concessions, build-operate-transfer agreements, and, finally, divestitures. The IIFC will work together with the line ministries to address such questions as:

- What is the goal of the private sector participation arrangement—new capacity, new technology, wider distribution, or other improvements?

- Are the necessary political and stakeholder support systems in place, along with mechanisms for cost recovery, knowledge of existing infrastructure, an adequate regulatory framework, and appropriate sources of finance?

- What would be the best private sector participation option?

- What is needed in terms of assistance with concession design and the tendering and negotiation of a formal arrangement with the private sector?

Infrastructure Development Company Limited

The Infrastructure Development Company Limited (IDCOL) is a nonbank financial institution. It was established in Bangladesh in 1997 as a government-owned limited company. The board of directors is comprised of senior government officials and prominent private sector entrepreneurs. A team of project financial advisors assists this group.

The IDCOL's objective is to promote significant participation of the private sector in investment, operation, ownership, and maintenance of infrastructure facilities. The government of Bangladesh and the World Bank fund IDCOL, which has access to roughly US$225 million. The organization has garnered interest from other international agencies that are willing to provide additional funds if sufficient demand is realized. The intent of IDCOL is to participate as a lender in limited recourse project finance, based on satisfactory evaluation of all aspects of the projects, in conjunction with the private sector. Its specific focus is the infrastructure sectors, including telecommunications, ports, toll roads, and other logistics infrastructure as may be approved by the government of Bangladesh.

IDCOL will finance up to 40 percent of the total costs of the build-own-operate and build-operate-transfer types of projects. The sponsor must have 20 percent of the equity for the total capital contribution.

Current projects in IDCOL's pipeline total an estimated total US$1.1 billion, including various energy projects valued at $672 million, the $200 million Stevedoring Services of America, Bangladesh (SSAB) container port, and the estimated $200 million Bangladesh Telephone and Telegraph Board's (BTTB) 300,000 telephone lines.

West Bengal Infrastructure Development Corporation

The West Bengal Infrastructure Development Corporation Ltd. (I-WIN) is a joint venture between the All India Public Financial Institution, ICICI Limited (formerly the Industrial Credit and Investment Corporation of India), and the state government owned West Bengal Industrial Development Corporation Ltd. (WBIDC). I-WIN was formed in 1995 with the objective of promoting

and facilitating infrastructure development in the state of West Bengal in India. It began operations in 1997. Its equity structure is comprised of 76 percent from ICICI and 24 percent from WBIDC. The board of directors includes professionals from ICICI and the state government. I-WIN participates in the following activities:

- Identifying suitable infrastructure projects for development, including the preparation of project feasibility reports and proposals for suitable financial structuring, mode of implementation, and appropriate ownership arrangements (such as the spectrum between purely private and purely public).

- Marketing properly packaged projects to potential domestic and international investors.

- Evaluating proposals for setting up infrastructure projects and assessing the competence of sponsors.

- Arranging finance for projects—equity, loans, and guarantees from the government, private sector, financial institutions, banks, and multilateral agencies.

- Providing project management services to selected projects.

- Advising the government on legal and regulatory reforms required to facilitate the flow of investments into projects.

Development efforts for the transportation infrastructure are focused on the following segments: roads and expressways, urban transportation and integrated area development, industrial parks, ports, waterways, and airports.

I-WIN also arranges requisite financing for infrastructure projects. Investments in Haldia include a major water supply project, internal roads, drainage, sewerage, and solid waste management systems, and commercial complexes. I-WIN is also involved in representing the state government's interest in a limited-access expressway that will connect Haldia, West Bengal, to the northern gateway city of Siliguri (in the northern part of West Bengal).

ORGANIZATIONS FOR PRIVATE OPERATIONS OF TRANSPORT INFRASTRUCTURE AND OPERATIONS

Under this emerging investment environment there have been several private-public partnerships in transport infrastructure and services traditionally restricted to the public sector. Examples of such initiatives include the contracting of operation and maintenance of the Jamuna Bridge in Bangladesh, the leasing contracts between Bangladesh Railways and the private sector, and a proposal for private development and operation of the port of Patenga in Bangladesh.

Jamuna Bridge Toll Operations

The concept of constructing the Jamuna Bridge began in 1964, seven years before the establishment of the Bangladeshi republic. The bridge was completed and became operational in June 1998 and was renamed the Bangabandhu Bridge. This is a multipurpose bridge providing road, rail, and gas connections between the physically divided regions.

A tender for private operation and management was awarded to an international joint venture consortium formed from South African, United Kingdom, and Bangladeshi corporations in June 1998. The contract involves the upkeep of all existing facilities, including roads, river, bridges, buildings, and equipment, as well as traffic management and the collection of tolls. The responsibilities include providing a maintenance management system, overseeing inspections of the main bridge structure and the east and west approach road, and routine maintenance inspections for the main bridge, river training, and highway structures.

This operation and maintenance five-year contract with the Jamuna Multipurpose Bridge Authority is based on a fixed fee to cover the provision of all defined services in the authority's area. Ownership, investment, and commercial risk reside with the government. The advantage of this arrangement for the government and the region is that the foreign private sector operator brings experience and foreign technology to the region, which may not have been feasible in a public arrangement.

Bangladesh Railway

Bangladesh Railway has involved the private sector in various initiatives to become more efficient, market-oriented, and financially self-sustaining. The efforts are aimed at enhancing productivity, improving service quality, and providing flexibility in the management of assets through leasing and BOT arrangements with the private sector. Among the initiatives are:

- Leasing out commercial activities of passenger trains on a 16-kilometer section connecting Dhaka to Narayanganj. This is a passenger service for commuters between Dhaka and Narayanganj daily. This section was leased out on July 7, 1997, to a private operator who took over the commercial activities of the passenger trains running between this section. The result was an increase in revenues of roughly 90 percent. In August 1998, the commercial activities (including ticketing and luggage booking) of Padmagarh Express, which runs between Santahar and Lalmonirhat, were also leased, producing a 368 percent increase in revenues.

- Leasing onboard services of the prestigious nonstop Subarna Express, which runs between Dhaka and Chittagong. As per the 1998 agreement, the lessee is responsible for the cleanliness of the coach, including toilets, passenger comfort, and safety. The staff posted by the private contractor ensures that only genuine passengers board the train, operates the public address system, and looks after any passenger requirements during the run. The lessee is permitted to run a pantry and buffet car, and to serve snacks, tea, and mineral water at a prefixed rate to the passengers. Bangladesh Railway pays service charges to the contractor after adjusting for the revenues from the pantry and buffet car. This agreement has assured better quality of service to the traveling public. Encouraged by the improvement in service quality, the railway intends to offer similar arrangements for a number of intercity trains running between important town and district centers.

- Leasing out of surplus capacity of Bangladesh Railway's fiber optic telephone system to a private phone company, Grameen Phone Ltd. (GP), on a long-term basis. As per this 1997 lease, GP assumes all relevant costs for the repair, replacement, operation, and maintenance of the railway telecommunication system, including paying the salaries of personnel engaged in this system. GP pays an annual rental for the lease to Bangladesh Railway. GP also repaired and upgraded the network and paid for the redundancies to improve the reliability of the system. The results of this partnership are the generation of revenues from the surplus capacity of the fiber optic telephone system and the added social benefit of increased telecommunication services at better prices.

- Private sector participation in a build-operate-transfer arrangement to upgrade non-

airconditioned cars. Bangladesh Railway's main constraint for modernizing its fleet has been inadequate funds for procurement and repairs. Intercity train distance between any two main city centers is about 300 to 400 kilometers, but none of the intercity trains have air-conditioned cars for these five-hour journeys. Air-conditioned buses plying the same routes have very competitive fares and are able to attract passengers away from the railroad. Under this arrangement, the private party will convert these coaches at their cost, improve their décor and interiors, and maintain them for the next four years. Bangladesh Railway will run the coaches in two intercity trains between Dhaka-Chittagong and Dhaka-Sylhet. The conversion of these coaches will be done in the railway workshop where the private party will bring its own equipment, material, and manpower. It will also train railway personnel in this conversion work. Bangladesh Railway will benefit by getting state-of-the-art technology at no initial cost and will get increased revenues due to the superior class of service provided to the traveling public.

- The Indian Railways have made similar arrangements, but these have been primarily limited to services on passenger coaches.

Port Development

In the mid 1990s, Orient Maritime Limited (a local ship chartering company and subsidiary of OPSIN Chemicals) and Stevedoring Services of America (an international terminal operator), proposed developing a second container seaport terminal for the Bangladesh market in Patenga south of the existing terminal in Chittagong Port. In December 1997, the Ministry of Shipping granted a concession on an unsolicited basis to SSAB, a joint-venture company owned equally by Orient Maritime and Stevedoring Services. The terms included the exclusive right to develop and operate the project for a 99-year tenure with an option to renew for another 99 years. As the container market for the proposed Patenga container terminal is close to Dhaka, the consortium pursued another proposal to develop and operate an ICD at Panagaon, in the vicinity of Dhaka. The intent was to complement the Patenga terminal by linking to the ICD with an inland waterway barge system. The Bangladesh Inland Waterway Transport Authority accepted this second proposal in 1998.

The proposal calls for an expenditure of about $220 million to build the terminal on a 50-acre site. The terminal will be capable of handling 300,000 TEU per year initially and, eventually, 600,000 TEU per year. At first, a break-bulk trucking system will be used to serve the Dhaka market. But when the ICD at Panagaon is ready, a barge system will carry the containers between the two terminals.

So far no approval has been given to develop the project, but negotiations are currently underway between the Ministry of Shipping and SSAB. The Ministry receives project advice from the IIFC while SSAB is receiving support from IDCOL.

FUTURE OF PRIVATE-PUBLIC PARTNERSHIP IN THE REGION

As the economies in the subregion develop and expand, significant capital will be required to finance transport projects to keep pace with the demand for infrastructure. Attracting capital from the private sector will be a major task. The governments need to consider more seriously the type of environment needed to attract foreign sources of capital. Because many of the projects call for limited recourse financing with its attendant risks, government officials must create an enabling environment that will be acceptable to investors.

There are many international lessons to be learned, whether the project is full-scale privatization, build-own-transfer, or a variation of the two (or based on leases or service contracts, especially after the explosion of private sector involvement in infrastructure services in East Asia and elsewhere in the 1990s). For every project that gets completed there are as many as four to five others that fail in the implementation process.[1] The reasons most often cited include underestimation of corruption, bureaucratic delays, and organized crime.

Even without these unconventional risks, typical infrastructure projects have complicated processes and long cycle times. Project developers have to:

- Establish the potential of the project;

- Identify the relevant decisionmakers;

- Determine the official procedures to steer the project through the approval process;

- Conduct economic, legal, financial, and engineering reviews;

- Prepare bidding documents and proposals;

- Obtain the relevant approvals, permits, and licenses;

- Structure the ownership of the project;

- Negotiate with lenders;

1.The Financial Times on March 11, 1999, commented on a survey of 7,500 multinational firms, of which 84 percent did not meet their financial targets for the last three years and 26 percent eventually failed.

- Select a contractor to build the project; and

- Choose an operator for the facility.

Some of the things that governments need to avoid if they are to develop a good reputation with the investment community include:

- Lack of a strong institutional framework that can lead to poor coordination and disagreement among government agencies whose approvals and clearances are required. A particular problem is the absence of a single authority to control the process.

- Poor institutional capacity due to a shortfall in expertise in private infrastructure projects. Although civil servants involved in publicly financed turnkey projects tend to be highly skilled in the engineering aspects of the projects, they lack the legal and financial skills to manage a complicated project structure such as a build-operate-transfer (BOT).

- Lack of transparency in the selection process due to insufficient experience and political cronyism that often leads to over-reliance on unsolicited proposals. Although unsolicited proposals that are correctly executed have merit, particularly in terms of speed and directness in developing projects, they lack the transparency, market orientation, and potential efficiency gains of competitive bidding.

- Market inefficiency that occurs when a government privatizes a project or liberalizes a sector without paying sufficient attention to the type of market it is creating. Governments frequently fail to establish an effective regulatory framework for protecting the public interest.

- Policy reversal that occurs when the commitments made by a previous government are not honored by the current government. The project developer at best is forced back to the negotiating table or, at worst, faces cancellation of the contract.

There is no particular road map for an effective policy framework to avoid the problems encountered in a public-private partnership. Each country has its own economic, social, and political circumstances and must develop its own solutions. Nevertheless, private sector projects are commonly judged on the basis of the ease or difficulty with which they are taken through the project cycle. The cycle consists of contract signing (such as concession or BOT), financial closure, permit and license approvals, project construction, sustainable operations, and responsiveness to consumer needs. Governments need to establish:

- An enabling environment that is transparent and consistent,

- A sound legal framework to assure the investment community concerning the rules of the game,

- A cadre of civil servants with the skills to implement private sector projects,

- Effective regulatory procedures to deal with market imperfections after privatization, and

- A sustainable commitment.

5

Setting a
Dynamic
Process
in Motion

Recent trends in globalization that enable the decentralization of production and distribution activities worldwide offer tremendous economic opportunities of employment and growth to poor countries. One-third of world trade in the mid 1990s occurred within such global production networks (World Bank 1999).[1] The ability of countries to grow rapidly depends on their capacity to link with global and regional markets. In turn, this capacity depends significantly on connectivity, and on the efficiency and speed with which goods and services can be moved from production centers to final markets.

One of the underlying objectives of this study was to develop ways to improve access to the landlocked areas of South Asia, specifically Nepal, Bhutan, and Northeast India. This objective is closely linked to opening up a region to new economic opportunity because of geographic interdependencies. For this reason, the study took a regional approach and focused on multicountry routes serving these areas. The conclusions for improving the trade logistics among these countries and with the outside world can also be applied to internal trade between the rural areas and the urban markets. The approach was to gather information from private sector logistics providers and shippers concerning the current situation on selected routes. The conclusions presented in this chapter for improving logistics will provide direct savings to the shippers, logistics providers, and consignees.

There are two fundamental questions. First, to what extent do the economies of the transit countries benefit from these improvements? Second, to what extent do these improvements benefit the poorer members of society? There are, of course, simple answers to these two questions. First, the country providing the transport infrastructure can recover its investment through appropriate charges to the transit vehicles and cargo while deriving additional value from complementary services provided to these transport activities. The value added is greatest where the transit country provides an efficient international

---

1. *World Development Report* 1999, The World Bank.

seaport gateway and some of the trucking or rail services used in the logistics chain. Second, the poorer sections of the society will derive direct benefits because of better access to urban and foreign markets for local products as well as increased employment associated with upgrading the transport infrastructure. The indirect benefits are the continuity of employment in industries, which, without better logistics, would lose market share. The more complex answers about the extent and allocation of benefits are dependent on the following issues:

- How well the isolated or landlocked regions are served,

- The structure of the charges (in terms of who pays and who benefits), and

- The efficiency of the logistic systems that will help minimize cost to the economy.

This chapter discusses the role of the Bank in helping to shape the outcome.

The previous sections made the following recommendations regarding transport and logistics in the subregion:

- **Protocols.** Establish or amend bilateral transit protocols to allow for the movement of transit cargo across borders under bond without transshipment or inspection.

- **Procedures.** Simplify and standardize the documents and clearance procedures required for cargo crossing land borders or exported or imported through the seaports.

- **Productivity.** Improve the productivity of the seaports and the railway services to eliminate unnecessary delays. These measures can dramatically reduce the time that cargo spends in ports or on railways.

- **Privatization.** Expedite the transfer of responsibility for transport operations and services (but not necessarily infrastructure) from the public to the private sector.

- **Providers.** Reduce the level of regulation of the providers of third-party logistics in a way that will both encourage competition and allow for vertical integration of such services as transport, storage, consolidation, documentation, and clearance. Modern regulations should be introduced to govern the liabilities associated with the carriage of cargo by different modes.

- **Perishability.** Improve the quality of logistics by placing an emphasis on reducing delivery time, increasing reliability of delivery, and minimizing losses en route to enable local manufacturers to compete for the supply of perishable products.

- **Packaging.** Increase the use of containers for shipment of goods by developing ICDs that allow cargo to be stuffed and destuffed closer to the point of origin or the point of destination.

- **Flexibility.** Allow flexible routing for vehicles carrying transit cargo or imports through defined border crossings.

- **Cyber trade.** Introduce electronic data interchange and business-to-business e-commerce to reduce logistics costs and time and overall transaction costs.

The changes that offer the largest benefits in terms of improved logistics are the revision of the current bilateral transit protocols, flexibility in transit cargo routing, and the increase in productivity at the seaports. Those offering significant benefits for both transit traffic and domestic traffic are improvements in the productivity of the railways and privatization of the transport services. The improvements in packaging, deregulation of logistics providers, and expansion of cyber trade offer the best long-term opportunities for reducing transaction costs and providing the quality of logistics required for high-value cargoes.

Improvements in transport logistics have important implications for poverty alleviation in one of the poorest regions of the world. This is possible through opening up the region and by offering new opportunities through better market linkages, easier and cheaper development of the resource base, and reduced losses that result from inefficient storage and multiple handling. The role of transportation in economic development includes everything from limited-access national highways to local feeder roads in rural areas, regional container transshipment terminals to barge terminals, and block trains to scheduled freight rail services. The same applies to logistics, which covers the complete movement from origin to destination. Improved logistics are especially important for small and medium industries in rural areas that must deliver a quality product within an acceptable time and at a competitive cost. Presented below are some examples in which the countries and states in the subregion are beginning to seek and find benefits of improved transport logistics.

Bhutan has recently explored the possibility of exporting fruits and vegetables and associated processed products. Although the industry has had some difficulties providing products of sufficient quality to sell in the neighboring countries, the major impediment has been poor inefficient transport links. Current border-crossing procedures create delays and add costs because of informal payments and damage to the perishable cargo. The future development of this trade will depend on better marketing and improved logistics.

The development of improved logistics within the region will encourage the growth in international and intraregional trade, as well as domestic trade between rural and urban areas. An example of the latter is the marketing of pumpkins produced along the river in the Bogra area. The pumpkins were formerly produced by poor people on public land and traded in the local market. Recent improvements in transportation that came about because of the construction of the Jamuna Bridge are now allowing the growers to sell their produce in urban markets.

The recently established Numaligarh refinery in Assam is examining ways to supply petroleum products to the Baghabari region in Bangladesh by transporting them to West Bengal via Bangladesh by inland waterways. The Indian refineries are located close to the Bramhaputra river (designated as the No. 2 National Waterway in India). The Inland Water Transit and Trade protocol between India and Bangladesh, revised in October 1999, facilitates easier and more rational barge movements between the two countries. Baghabari would be the port of call for Indian vessels for unloading petroleum products because large storage facilities and barge unloading facilities already exist.

STRATEGIC LINKAGES AND AREAS FOR DEVELOPMENT

The previous chapters examined various routes requiring additional development. Other routes were selected based on the findings of background studies conducted under the Regional Initiative and other projects (such as the Nepal Multimodal Trade and Transit Facilitation Project and the Export Diversification Project) and observations of the private sector. From these, a core set of strategic linkages or routes have been identified that would create opportunities for increased economic growth and trade in the subregion. These would include:

The key routes linking landlocked Nepal and Bhutan to regional and international markets include:

- Kathmandu-Birgunj-Calcutta

- Kathmandu-Bhairahwa-Nhava Sheva

- Kakarbhitta-Phulbari-Banglbandh-Dhaka

- Thimphu-Phuntsoling-Siliguri-Calcutta

- Thimphu-Phuntsoling-Burimari-Dhaka

The key routes linking the Northeast states of India to regional and international markets would include:

- Calcutta-Benapole-Akhaura-Agartala (road and rail)

- Calcutta-Gede-Darsena-Jamuna Bridge-Akhaura-Agartala

- Agartala-Akhaura-Chittagong

The routes linking the landlocked countries are currently used but are inefficient due to problems at the border crossings and seaports. The exception is one of the more efficient ports at Nhava Sheva. These routes require improvements in both roads and port operations. They would also benefit from changes in customs procedures and revisions of the bilateral transit protocols. The routes to Northeast India are not currently used because they lack critical links and are not designated as transit routes in the bilateral agreements. These will require a combination of investment and revision of the agreements.

The most immediate problem affecting the efficiency of shipments of imports, exports, and transit cargoes is the productivity of the ports. Cumbersome operating procedures, restrictive work rules, old and unreliable equipment, and a lack of commercial management produce long, unnecessary, and unpredictable delays. In addition, they add to the informal payments and the loss of cargo. These not only account for a significant portion of the time and cost for land transport, but they also add to the ocean freight costs by delaying vessels and discouraging the use of larger vessels and scheduled shipping services.

Calcutta faces the additional problems of siltation and a location more than 100 kilometers up the Hooghly River. Investments in container facilities and equipment in recent years have not been able to offset the problems associated with low labor productivity and limited depth at the berth. Chittagong has problems of road access for containers moving to and from Dhaka. It also has difficulties with labor productivity that remain despite investments in new facilities and equipment. Any attempt to reduce the delays and costs to cargo moving through these ports must first address management problems and the low rate of utilization of existing assets.

The second most important problem is the lack of capacity and efficiency at the border crossings. It is important to establish a set of border crossings capable of handling trucks and rail traffic that do not cause unnecessary delays because of inadequate facilities, poor management, and complex procedures. The number of these border crossings should be limited in order to reduce the cost of establishing and staffing these crossings and, more importantly, to ensure that there is a sufficient concentration of traffic to attract private sector providers of logistics services such as freight forwarding, customs clearance, and banking. Table 5.1 lists the primary border crossings and their key constraints.

The scale of operation at the border crossings can be categorized as:

- High-volume operations such as Benapole with a significant volume of traffic in both

TABLE 5.1   CONSTRAINTS AT BORDER CROSSINGS AND PORTS

Border crossing	Mode	Problem	Action
Chittagong	Water	Inefficient management and operations, lack of equipment, excessive delays and costs	Privatization of port operations and investment
Calcutta	Water	Inefficient management and operations, lack of equipment, excessive delays and costs	Privatization of port operations and investment (increased use of Haldia for Nepal)
Benapole/Petrapol	Road	Congestion	Construction; simplify procedures
Birgunj/Rauxal	Rail	Operations not yet decided	Privatize ICD operations
Bhairahwa/Notanawa	Road	Operations not yet decided	Privatize ICD operations
Benapole/Petrapol	Rail	Soon to start operations	Simplify procedures
Darsana/Gede	Rail	Long processing times	Simplify procedures. Bank and custom to be available seven days per week
Akhaura/Agartala	Road/ rail	Not open for traffic	Protocol for road and rail movement
Kakarbhitta- Panitanki	Road	Poor facilities on both borders, no customs at Banglaband	Improve border crossing facilities; allow transit for Nepalese trucks
Burimari-Changrabaandh	Road	Insufficient infrastructure, lack of customs office, bad road access	Infrastructure investments

Source: Logistics cost study team, World Bank.

directions, including both import/export and transit cargoes. These crossings require adequate parking area for the vehicles, warehousing for cargo that is stored while waiting for documents, loading platforms for inspection of cargo and for transit shipment, and fully equipped customs checkpoint gates.

- Medium-volume operations such as Burimari that handle both import/export and transit cargoes. This crossing requires storage and parking areas as well as customs checkpoints, but on a smaller scale than a high-volume operation.

- Low-volume operations such as Banglabandh with traffic limited to transit cargo that is ei-

ther traveling in-bond under seal or has been precleared. This cargo requires only a road crossing from one country to the other with a checkpoint to verify the seal or confirm that the cargo has been cleared.

The first group of border crossings is relatively expensive to develop. The crossings require large areas for storage of vehicles or rail wagons to meet demand during peak flows and periods when there is a disruption to normal activity at the border crossing. The volume of traffic and the average processing time for customs determines the amount of warehousing and inspection facilities. The customs checkpoints should have a sufficient number of parallel gates to accommodate the normal weekly peak. The gates should have air-conditioned offices equipped with communications equipment. Where appropriate, they may also be equipped with an automatic weighbridge. Space should be provided for the addition of new gates as traffic increases. Over time, as procedures are simplified and the number of inspections are reduced, the amount of facilities required will decrease. The increasing percentage of the cargo that moves directly across the border without handling or storage will offset the increase in traffic.

The access road to the border crossings should have sufficient width and the bridges should have sufficient strength to accommodate fully loaded trucks, including tractor-trailers. The road should widen as it approaches the checkpoint to create a waiting area large enough to handle the normal weekly peak traffic. Public investment in these border crossings should be limited to the customs facilities, such as the checkpoint and inspection area, as well as to the road or rail access. The private sector should develop the remainder of the infrastructure, such as warehousing, office space, and, possibly, parking areas.

Where possible, the customs facilities on both sides of the border should be located in a common structure and the processing should be done at the same time. If this is not possible, the opposing checkpoints should be established with a minimum distance between them and be linked by dedicated telephone and data channels. These would allow the customs officials on one side to advise the officials on the other side of information about a vehicle crossing the border.

POLICY REFORM AND IMPROVED TRANSIT PROTOCOLS

It is important to simplify the procedures for clearing vehicles and their cargo at the land border

crossings and at the seaports. The resulting increase in productivity will minimize investment in facilities and storage as well as the cost of staffing and operations. This simplification should begin with the development of a common format for the basic import/export and transit cargo declarations. A common document should be adopted for the four countries within SAARC in order to expedite the exchange of information between officials on each side of a border. The basis for this common structure has already been initiated by the decision of Bangladesh, Bhutan, and Nepal to use the ASYCUDA format for trade information. India has decided to use a proprietary format that is supposed to be compatible with ASYCUDA.

The common declaration form should be in a format that can be computerized so that the data can be easily transferred between customs checkpoints. The processing of this document should be simplified to minimize the number of signatures and copies required for clearing cargo. This form should be developed in conjunction with efforts to establish a national electronic data interchange (EDI) system. Although it is unlikely that a full-scale EDI system will be available for cross-border movements anytime in the near future, such a system will be introduced fairly soon in airports and seaports. The EDI system should also be expandable to the land border crossings, and the data entry system should provide an interface for trucking companies and railroads, as well as for airlines and shipping lines.

The existing bilateral agreements between each of the neighboring countries in the region are only a preliminary step toward the free movement of goods across borders and through countries to gateway ports. The major problems with these agreements are that they attempt to restrict the number of routes and impose cumbersome customs procedures on both bilateral trade and transit cargoes. In amending these protocols, it is necessary to allow greater flexibility in the routing of transit cargo and to simplify cross-border procedures to reflect the efficient practices achieved elsewhere in Asia.

The problem of existing protocols is that they do not allow for unhindered movement of trucks and railway wagons across national boundaries. At the extreme, they prohibit such movements. At a minimum, they subject the vehicles and their cargo to lengthy clearance procedures even for transit cargo moving from border to border or border to seaport. One of the difficulties in developing better protocols is that the transit countries do not perceive any immediate benefits for themselves, but they do perceive security risks. Although the continuing efforts at trade liberalization and economic reform are reducing the incentives for illegal movement of goods across borders, the maintenance of secure borders remains a priority for customs authorities. Furthermore, each of the countries in the region has difficulties in providing adequate transport infrastructure for its own use and is reluctant to improve infrastructure and allow free access for adjoining countries.

The procedural problems in allowing relatively unhindered movement of transit goods across the border have been resolved by various customs unions and trade blocs throughout the world, but the mechanism of cost recovery has not. An earlier work by the Bank[2] suggested that the transit country obtains considerable value-added benefits in providing support services for transit movements, but the primary benefit is the participation of the transport industries in the transit countries. In lieu of such participation, it is reasonable to collect a fee for the use of the infrastructure. It is also necessary to enforce regional and domestic regulations that will ensure safe operation and accountability of the transit vehicles. Although there are ongoing discussions regarding these issues, it is important to accelerate these initiatives and to take full advantage of international experience in resolving these issues.

Among the procedures that have been introduced throughout the world over the last decade and a half are:

- International standards for the documents used for the movement of transit goods across multiple borders,

- Replacement of hard-copy documents with EDI,

- New mechanisms for securing transit cargo to prevent it from being sold in the local economy,

- New techniques for tracking shipments to prevent the loss of cargo equipment in transit,

- New methods of inspection to eliminate delays and irregularities, and

- Improved communications between customs authorities both to facilitate cross-border movements and to identify irregularities.

MODERNIZATION OF TRANSPORT NETWORKS AND SERVICES

The plans for improving the national transport networks in each of the four countries need to address problems of capacity and quality of the existing networks as well as the need for expansion of the networks' coverage. Both investments and policy reforms are required. A number of initiatives are planned to improve currently used

---

2. G. Ollivier and P. N. Taborga "Development of Trade Services." Working Paper, Infrastructure Unit in Europe and Central Asia, World Bank, 1999.

routes and introduce alternative ones. To date, the efforts to develop efficient and effective transport networks in the four countries have not been completely successful. However, there are encouraging signs that recent initiatives will be more successful. The proposal to develop a golden quadrilateral of dual carriageway roads connecting the largest cities in India is an important step toward addressing the very serious problem of capacity shortages on the national road network. The investment in broad-gauge and dual-gauge track will expand railroad services and reduce rail costs for eastern Bangladesh and Northeastern India.

The conversion of the rail network to broad gauge and improvements in cross-border procedures offer the potential for a significant increase in rail's market share. This is strengthened by the growing congestion and poor maintenance of the road network, which have already eliminated the speed advantage of trucks. The increase in rail's market share will be primarily low- to medium-value cargo, especially cement, coal, boulders, and other bulk cargoes moving in large consignments.

There will also be some increase in rail's market share of container movements because of the growth in unit train operations and the expansion in Concor's operations. Better rail service will attract more boxes in areas where there is sufficient volume to justify dedicated rail ICDs. As an example, the development of a rail ICD at Birgunj will extend the handling of containers to the border and make the route to Nhava Sheva more attractive. If there is sufficient traffic volume when the broad-gauge rail connections are completed to Birgunj, unit trains could become the preferred mode for movement of high-value cargo to and from Nepal. If the new road from Kathmandu to the border that was proposed in the 1980s were to finally be constructed, then the possibility for container movements into

Nepal could dramatically change the economics of all routes to and from Nepal. The role of railroads in container transport could be greatly enhanced if Indian Railways were to make unit train operations available to major multimodal operators such as Maersk and Neptune Orient Lines (NOL). Also, if container operations could be extended to Bangladesh, the potential for moving high-value cargo, such as yarn, would increase quality assurance and reduce delays.

The critical investments for the rail network are gauge harmonization on the primary routes, procuring rolling stock for high-speed container block trains, and establishing ICDs. The former would include the extension of the dual-gauge rail in Bangladesh from the Jamuna Bridge to Dhaka, Tongi, Akhaura, and on to Chittagong, and in India up to the Nepal border ICDs. It would eliminate costly transshipments and enhance the comparative advantage of rail for medium and long distances. The ICDs would be established in Northeast India to provide container movements to the rest of India. These would provide efficient transfer of containers between modes and serve as repositioning centers for empty containers to be stuffed.

The growing congestion on the Indian roads not only reduces average travel speeds but also creates greater variance in travel times. This is expected to slow the growth in road's share of cargo movement. The expressway proposed by the Asian Development Bank from Haldia and Calcutta to Siliguri would reduce the travel time by truck, but it would not solve the problem of seaport delays. If the government is able to overcome union opposition and improve the performance of Haldia and Calcutta, more traffic will be attracted to these ports, especially cargo headed to Asia. Without significant improvements in these ports, the expressway will provide an attractive connection via the golden quadrangle to Nhava Sheva or Chennai.

The essential investments for the road network are widening the primary road links and strengthening the bridges along those routes. This would significantly reduce the cost of transport by allowing larger vehicles to operate on the roads and allow the maintenance of higher average speeds so that these vehicles will be better utilized. The major routes that are being widened and upgraded are the Golden Quadrilateral in India and the expressway from Haldia to Siliguri. In Bangladesh, the road from Chittagong to Dhaka is being upgraded.[3] The links eastward to Akhoura and Agartala and westward through Benapole to Calcutta are critical links that also require upgrading.

Investments in ICDs and landports also deserve special attention. This includes (a) the completion of the ICDs along the Nepal border and their conversion to private operation, (b) the expansion of the Benapole crossing with an orientation toward increasing productivity and reducing delays rather than merely adding capacity, (c) the improvements in facilities and protocol for containers moving between Bhairahwa and Moradabad, and (d) the development of new ICDs to transfer import/export containers moving to and from Bhutan and Northeast India. The economic viability of an ICD at Siliguri would need to be examined. Within Bangladesh, Tongi in the east and Noapara in the west appear to be possible locations for ICDs.

The proposed development of a private container terminal at Patenga south of Chittagong with an inland water connection to a Dhaka ICD would offer a significant improvement over the slow and costly movement through the port of Chittagong. It would make the transit routes through Bangladesh more attractive for high-value cargo, especially as the port would not have the problem of heavy siltation. If a private port facility were available to the south of Calcutta with good road and rail connections, it would divert substantial traffic from Calcutta.

The introduction of effective in-bond movement of cargo with minimal delays at the border and an end to transshipments of cargo between vehicles will increase the volume of high-value import and export cargo to and from Nepal and Bhutan. It would also encourage traffic between Bangladesh and India.

For the inland waterway network, the most frequently mentioned infrastructure investments are increasing the depth in specific routes and improving navigational aids to allow for night navigation. The latter is more achievable in the short run and is necessary because of the very low average travel speeds. The former would be difficult to achieve because of the current condition of the dredging fleet. Moreover, it is not required for Class I routes, which include most of those under consideration for handling cross-border traffic.

None of the proposed investments in infrastructure will be successful without a mechanism for proper maintenance of the infrastructure and efficient operation of the transport services utilizing the infrastructure. Improvements in the management of the transport infrastructure are even more important than the proposed capital investments. The primary impediment to effective use of the existing transport services is a lack of commercial orientation on the part of the public sector responsible for providing services or developing infrastructure. The trucking industry is almost entirely private and relatively efficient. However, trucks are old and small because of the small size of consignments, competitive pressure on prices, poor condition of the roads,

---

3. The Asian Development Bank is financing the upgrade. In addition, Japanese financing has been used to upgrade some of the bridges along the route.

and lack of enforcement of vehicle safety regulations, including annual inspections and load limits. The government needs to address the last two constraints. The maintenance of the roads (in particular the primary routes) needs to be improved dramatically. This, combined with wider roads, will allow larger vehicles to compete with the older vehicles and thereby reduce the cost of road transport.

New approaches such as toll roads, road maintenance contracts, and road funds need to be introduced to address the perennial problem of pavement deterioration and excessive road roughness. The enforcement of existing laws would produce an initial increase in transport costs as older vehicles are disqualified from operations and the amount and extent of overloading is reduced, but it will reduce the costs of accidents and increase the reliability of road transport. At the same time, it will generate mutual trust between countries regarding the safety of the trucks crossing over the border.[4]

The railroad industry remains almost entirely under the control of the public sector. The private sector manages some stations or train services on some of the less utilized routes. At the same time, there has been the largely successful effort in India to create a parastatal container rail haulage company, Concor. Despite the rapid growth in container shipments, much more needs to be done. In Bangladesh, the use of unit trains for movement of containers is much more limited. The only service is between Chittagong and the ICD in Dhaka. It handles a very small portion of the loaded box movements. Despite perennial efforts by the major shipping lines to establish their own block train operations, the railroads of both countries have been unwilling to enter any agreements. The rail sector requires competitive services if it is to stabilize its market share.

One of the more interesting proposals for private investment and management of infrastructure and related services is the proposal to establish a container port at Patenga, Bangladesh. The port would be operated with a new ICD in Dhaka and connected by a container-on-barge service. The proponent of the port would provide and operate both facilities, thereby solving three problems: excessive port delays, limitations on truck size, and inefficient unit train operations. When the Dhaka-Chittagong highway is widened, the bridges strengthened, and rail and ICD operations improved, the movement of containers could be split more evenly among the three modes.

The four countries under discussion each have made significant advancements in liberalizing their economies and their trade policies. Both India and Bangladesh have joined the World Trade Organization. All have made concerted efforts to reduce the involvement of government in commercial activities and to create a more competitive transport sector with an emphasis on private sector operations. The amount of change is impressive when compared to the decades during which the governments focused on protecting their economies from outside competition and emphasized the role of the public sector in regulating commercial activities. Perhaps nowhere in the region is this change more evident than in India's software industry. In a relatively short time, the country has been able to establish a strong, internationally competitive industry by taking advantage of local skills and allowing for competitive forces to dictate the development of the sector.[5] The success of this

---

4. The United States has recently used the argument of safety to exclude Mexican trucks from U.S. highways despite the NAFTA agreements. This form of implicit protectionism, reminiscent of similar U.S. arguments regarding flag-of-convenience vessels, should be avoided in SAARC.

5. Recent attempts by the government to introduce some form of regulation of the sector have met with extremely strong resistance from all sectors.

sector depends on efficient logistics. The software industry has taken advantage of modern telecommunications (bypassing the less efficient telephone monopoly) to reduce the cost and time of the logistics chain, thereby significantly reducing transaction costs. This has allowed private industry to mobilize its considerable intellectual resources to produce, market, and sell high-value tradable goods.

Similar changes will be required if the manufacture of garments, textiles, and yarn, the region's major export industry, is to remain competitive. So far, Nepal, India, and Bangladesh have used their comparative advantage in labor costs to produce garments for the low end of the market. They have strengthened their competitive position through experience with modern manufacturing techniques and the mobilization of domestic financing. In particular, Bangladesh and Nepal have seen a rapid growth in their exports of ready-made garments. Although intraregional trade is expected to grow as these industries direct their design and production activities toward local markets, the extraregional trade is expected to face increasing competition from China and underdeveloped countries in Southeast Asia. Once the international system of quotas is eliminated, future growth of exports from India, Bhutan, and Nepal will depend on the ability to move toward higher quality, limited run, and end products.

At the same time, the high end of the market is undergoing dramatic change. A larger segment of the market is requiring better quality and design. Computerization of the design, pattern preparation, sewing, and embroidery of garments allows countries with higher cost labor to produce better quality garments at costs that are comparable to production in low-wage countries. It also allows efficient production of the smaller size orders with more frequent changes in design that are needed to meet the requirements for changing fashion. In the next decade, it is

expected that body scanners and databases will replace traditional measurements, thus blurring the distinction between ready-made and tailored garments. Increasingly, garments will be direct ordered by the consumer with marketing and sales through the Internet. Although these changes have only just begun to appear at the upper end of the market, it is reasonable to assume that they will be adopted very quickly across a wide customer base. In this evolving situation, efficient logistics will become a necessary complement to the technological innovations. In addition to putting competitive pressure on management, these changes will offer opportunities for workers in the industry to increase their skills and to earn higher wages.

CHANGES AFFECTING FUTURE LOGISTICS

The logistics chains that serve the external trade of the region are expected to undergo significant changes over the decade. Globalization, and all its implications for increased competition in traded goods, will require substantial improvements in logistics in order to maintain competitive advantage. Both the public and private sectors must be involved in efforts to improve logistics. Changes in transit protocols and reforms in customs require coordinated actions by neighboring governments. Changes in line-haul movements must combine actions by private sector truck operators and national railways. Improvements in port performance require increased private sector involvement in operations of public infrastructure.

Changes in Commodities Shipped

Chapter 1 reviewed the growth of foreign trade within the region. It indicated a rapid growth in the value of trade. Data from the seaports indicate a rapid growth in tonnage as well. Significant growth was also observed in intraregional trade (in terms of absolute value of trade).

In Nepal, the principal export-oriented industries are ready-made garments and carpets. The former recently exceeded carpets in terms of value of shipments. The major overseas markets for ready-made garments are the United States and Germany, although the latter has declined in importance as markets became saturated with Nepalese goods. The growth of exports has been constrained by problems with quality control, availability of skilled labor, competition from India, and poor logistics. Nepal has undeveloped mineral resources, but it remains a net importer of cement and raw materials for steelmaking. Imports include a wide variety of manufactured goods as well as textiles for the garment and carpet industry. India also accounts for about 45 percent of imports in terms of value. Trade with India has increased rapidly over the last seven years, and India is now Nepal's third largest trading partner.

The major exports of Bangladesh include ready-made garments, leather goods, jute and jute goods, and frozen foods, especially shrimp. The country has had problems with quality control for shrimp exports and with insufficient textile production to meet the demands of the garment industry. The major markets are the United States and Western Europe, which account for about one-third and one-fourth of the value of imports, respectively. Although exports have increased in recent years, growth has been below expectations. Despite improvements in the road and rail network, limited coverage, poor performance, and deterioration in service during the monsoon season handicap the country's transport system.

Bangladesh imports a wide variety of manufactured goods, of which textiles and related goods account for about 25 percent. India provides about one-sixth of the total value and East Asia accounts for about one-fourth. Improved relations with India have led to an increase in trade, which will continue as new routes to Northeast India are opened and road and rail movements across the western border improve. Although regional trade in basic commodities such as cement, grain, jute, and boulders will continue to be important, the future growth in trade with India is expected to be in medium- and high-value goods. Better logistics are urgently required for efficient truck movements across the border. If the road transport continues to suffer from congestion and the private sector participation in rail services increases, rail may provide the improved logistics.

India has experienced rapid growth in both imports and exports as a result of the liberalization of its trade policy. Traditional exports of cloth, garments, fibers, leather goods, animal feed, chemicals, and minerals have been broadened to include fish, gems, pharmaceuticals, and software. The primary destinations for Indian exports are Europe, which receives about 25 percent by value; the United States, which receives about 20 percent; and Japan and China, which each receive about 10 percent. Trade with the surrounding countries is primarily in food products, construction materials, and transport equipment, and it is now being supplemented with other consumer goods.

Imports have been increasing rapidly in response to boosting domestic production. The major imports are petroleum products, which account for more than 25 percent of the total value of imports, precious stones and metals, which account for over 15 percent, and chemicals, which account for about 12 percent. The remainder are primarily manufactured goods, most notably machinery and instruments, transport equipment, textiles, and food and food products.

The increase in trade in higher-value commodities is already putting pressure on the logistics services. Containerized shipments are increasing rapidly despite the limitations of the road network and the ports for accommodating containers. Air freight is becoming more important, as is electronic transfer of information technology materials. Rapid improvements in logistics will be critical to sustaining this growth in trade.

In the future, it is expected that exports of textiles will experience slow growth or even a decline as quota systems are dismantled and Indian manufacturers shift investments back to India. The manufacturing sectors that are expected to increase are pharmaceuticals that exploit local medicinal plants and household consumables that are sold in Indian markets. Nepal's ability to compete in both export markets and trade with India will depend on its capacity to delivery higher-value goods in a timely manner. A major effort is needed to improve container transport and extend the movement of boxes further into Nepal. Past efforts to improve the performance at the border and at Calcutta have had limited success. As a result, it is likely that there will be considerable diversion of exports to Nhava Sheva and other seaports that offer efficient container services.

Tighter Linkages between Suppliers and Buyers

The innovation in marketing and sales currently sweeping the developed world under the aegis of the Internet will soon make its impact felt in developing countries. E-commerce, in the form of both business-to-business and business-to-customer applications, will rapidly expand during the coming decade. These applications take advantage of modern communications and information processing to reduce the cost of access to and transactions between buyers and sellers. One of the areas in which e-commerce is expected to have the most profound impacts is in marketing and sales for small- to medium-sized enterprises located outside major urban areas.

The effectiveness of e-commerce depends on the quality of both communications and logistics. The ability to deliver products from sellers to buyers at low cost and in a timely manner requires efficient operations, not only for transport but also for packaging, labeling, storing/managing inventories, tracking, financing, and customs processing.

The logistics requirements are expected to change over time as the trade changes and as the transportation network evolves. New routes will be developed and market shares will change as the performance of different nodes and links change. The private sector participants in the major trades were asked for recommendations for new routes, which should be introduced to facilitate the movement of goods from landlocked areas. Consultants' reports focusing on different modes also produced a myriad of recommendations. This analysis has presented a means for evaluating alternatives. However, this becomes quite complex when considering different commodities and different foreign origins and destinations. Furthermore, trade is now evolving relatively rapidly, as are alternative multimodal routes. In this environment it is increasingly difficult for governments to respond rapidly to the changes in the marketplace. More and more, designated routes are becoming a constraint on trade rather than a facilitator. Although government involvement in trade facilitation remains essential, it is no longer beneficial for the public sector to restrict the mode and routing of cargo moving between border crossings or from border crossings to final destinations.

POSSIBLE IMPLICATIONS FOR BANK GROUP INVOLVEMENT

The array of instruments that are available to the Bank (and Bank Group) range from the lending, technical assistance, sector, and policy dialogue under the CAS framework to the emerging role as a knowledge bank, convenor, and partner with other institutions' resource mobilization responsibilities.

We have attempted to examine how the Bank might play a role in regional or multinational initiatives such as this one.[6] We have used a simple chart (Figure 5.1) that rates the key elements of the regional transport initiative on scales of ■ (low) to ■■■■■ (high) for three main criteria: (a) constraints, (b) benefits, and (c) the Bank's possible role.

Within each of these groups there are subcategories that provide more clarification. It is important to highlight that the ratings are notional ratings by the study team and are intended mainly to provide the basis for discussion with Bank staff and management.

The key constraints in the area of reducing logistics costs through improved trade facilitation systems, simplification of documentation, procedures, and other such measures are mainly institutional constraints that have the potential to have good impact or provide high benefits for increased international and intraregional trade. This is one area that would provide broad benefits to all concerned because it reduces the costs of doing business with low investment implications but high technical assistance needs. The Bank's role in its individual country operations, as well as all of its other instruments, could have a strong impact. The South Asia region has lending and technical assistance operations in trade facilitation in Nepal (Nepal Multimodal Transport and Trade Facilitation Project), and some aspects such as customs reform are being addressed in Bangladesh through the Export Diversification project. But such reforms are not being addressed in India and Bhutan. The Bank's

experience in global best practices in trade facilitation, harmonization and simplification of documentation, customs systems, policy reform, and transit procedural practices can be brought to the region through initiatives such as the Global Trade Facilitation partnership. The Bank also can play the role of a convenor, as done during the April 1999 Regional Technical Workshop on Transport and Transit Facilitation, and share global experiences.

In mode and route choice for more cost-effective transportation, political constraints and, to a slightly smaller extent, institutional constraints, have a strong influence. As Chapter 3 discussed, the political constraints here are linked to those of protocol, and shippers are constrained in their choices. The technical constraints in terms of compatibility of transport networks (such as rail gauge and load standards) and gaps in physical infrastructure networks are a somewhat lesser problem in the subregion. This is mainly because the roads are compatible and the rail problems are being corrected in Bangladesh and India. The bigger infrastructure inadequacies require long-term measures and investments. Some of these gaps are being addressed through country operations. The strategic impact of the operations, particularly on poverty, could be enhanced if the regional dimension could be more effectively and consistently integrated in country strategies. In the area of knowledge management, the Bank through advisory and analytic activity such as this one, can highlight options and provide a basis for rational decisionmaking in which the users of the systems can participate.

The third category of rationalizing bilateral and multilateral protocol is a politically sensitive area that has historically been addressed on a bilateral basis. The SAARC charter does not allow for SAARC intervention on bilateral issues. However, we have seen that several constraints in the transport logistics systems would require rationaliza-

---

6. The framework, of course, could also be adapted for the more traditional country operations and interaction.

FIGURE 5.1   CONNECTING THE SUBREGION: ECONOMIC GROWTH AND POVERTY ALLEVIATION

Category	Reducing logistics costs	Routes and modes for more cost-effective transport	Rationalizing bilateral/ regional protocol	Promoting private sector participation
Constraints				
Economic	■	■■	■■	■
Political	■	■■■■■	■■■■■	■■■
Technical	■■	■■■		
Institutional	■■■■■	■■■	■■■■	■■■■
Impacts				
Economic opportunities	■■■■■	■■■■■	■■■■■	■■■■■
Increased international, intraregional trade	■■■■■	■■■■■	■■■■■	■■■■■
Promote competition and increase efficiency	■■■■■	■■■■■	■■■■■	■■■■■
Bank Group's possible role				
Country operations through CAS/comprehensive development framework (lending, technical assistance, policy dialogue)	■■■■■	■■■■	■■	■■■■
Convenor	■■■■■	■■■		■■■■■
Resource mobilization and fiduciary	■■■■	■■■■		■■■■
Knowledge management, best practice cases, analytic advisory services	■■■■■	■■■■■	■■	■■■■■

Note: ■■■■■ indicates a high rating; ■■■ is medium; and ■ is low. The ratings are those of the study team and are notional, intended to provide the basis for discussion with Bank staff and management.
Source: Bank study team.

tion of the protocols and broader consultations with stakeholders, particularly those who are directly impacted (such as shippers and exporters in the case of transit protocol). When anomalies in protocol and agreements are reduced, there are significant gains, including increased trade, greater economic opportunities and improved efficiency through increased competition. The Bank's direct role is limited in this area. However, in our country operations and policy dialogue, specific issues can be flagged for consideration of the relevant countries. With the Bank's matrix management structure, this could be enabled with more dialogue between country management teams. Also the Bank, if requested, can help with "good practice" cases and in-depth policy inputs.

The final category of promoting private sector participation in dialogue with governments concerns regional transport issues. The constraints on investment and operations in transport, transshipment, and logistics services are mainly institutional. The critical need for involving the private sector is well understood and the positive impacts are undeniably large. The Bank operations in infrastructure projects, particularly water supply and sanitation, have been pushing the envelope on this for some time. In the transport sector, the experience with privatization has mainly been in ports rather than in the road and rail sectors. In trade facilitation and logistics, the attempts to include private sector organizations (such as chambers of commerce, freight forwarders' associations, and shippers' councils) in a more substantive manner have begun and can be strengthened. Also, ways of promoting and sup-porting private sector participation in provision and management of logistics services can be explored. On the knowledge management side, there is clear demand from the region for policy notes and for a forum for increased dialogue. One of the key recommendations that the public and private delegates of Bangladesh, Bhutan, India, and Nepal made at the regional technical workshop (which was again reiterated at national consultative meetings) was to establish regional committees with a mix of public and private sector representatives to promote more consistent and coherent dialogue. The private sector in the subregion has set up a four-country forum that would raise issues with the relevant governments.

Several international development and private sector agencies are involved in the region in such aspects as trade policy reform, highway improvements, toll roads, road maintenance funds, railroad improvements and privatization, port improvement and privatization, ICDs, EDI, and improved telecommunications. A more coherent effort to work in partnership with these agencies is critical for effective strategy and implementation.

6

Next:
Proposed Change

The primary goal of this study was not to identify new projects for investment or to provide a regional transport master plan for improved transportation and logistics net works. The problems discussed in this study have been the subject of discussion at the national and regional levels for a number of years, and the conclusions derived from the comparative analysis are consistent with the issues already raised by the private sector. Rather, our objective has been to develop a mechanism whereby the best efforts of government, the private sector, and international experience can be mobilized, and regional stakeholders can use the mechanism to identify and provide direction for solutions for these problems. Summary recommendations for consideration at national and regional levels are presented in Table 6.1. The solutions are important not only for improving current economic performance and developing areas where economic development has been lagging, but also to meet the challenges of the future when rapidly falling transaction costs and constantly improving logistics will change the nature of competitive advantage for both developed and developing countries.

Because many of the solutions involve policy matters and coordination between countries, an effective and sustainable mechanism by which such coordination can be achieved is important. One of the key recommendations of the delegates from the four countries at the World Bank/Economic and Social Commission for Asia and the Pacific April 1999 Regional Technical Workshop on Transport and Transit Facilitation (see proceedings of the workshop)[1] was to establish a regional technical working committee to examine and promote key subregional issues. Regional representation is critical because many of the solutions extend beyond national and bilateral issues. Technical expertise is critical because of the breadth of activities to be covered and the interdependent links among issues. This study confirms

1. Proceedings of the workshop can be obtained from the World Bank. Also available at the Bank's external website http://www.worldbank.org/html/fpd/transport/trfacil/present.htm.

TABLE 6.1   NATIONAL AND REGIONAL ACTIONS: SHORT TERM AND MEDIUM TO LONG TERM

National	Regional
Short Term	
1. Strengthen the Transport and Trade Facilitation Technical Committees (TTTCs) recently established in Bangladesh, Bhutan, and Nepal that are aimed at sustaining interaction between the public agencies and the private sector. These committees now include representation from ministries or departments of commerce, customs, and transport or communication, and private sector representation from chambers of commerce, transport service providers associations, and trade associations. Examine similar institutional options for increased effective dialogue on transport, logistics, and trade facilitation issues in India in the public and private sectors.	1. Establish a regional technical working committee to (a) identify methods for improving logistics for intraregional and extraregional trade, (b) set priorities and short-term targets for achieving the greatest benefits, and (c) develop a forceful and sustainable program for improving logistics in the region. The committee will include: • Government representatives of the relevant trade, transport, and customs agencies to provide the policy and public infrastructure perspective. • Private sector representatives from shippers, consignees, chambers of commerce, and logistics providers to bring a private sector and commercial perspective. • Specialists from other countries and academia representatives to provide best practices knowledge of trade facilitation, supply-chain management, and logistics services, as well as practical limitations on reforms experienced by other regional trade blocs.
2. Technical assistance should be provided to assist transport ministries, development banks, planning ministries, freight forwarders, major shippers, and experts in logistics in the techniques of supply-chain analysis. The logistics cost model developed would provide an easy and adaptable tool for training stakeholders. Procedures should be developed for incorporating supply-chain analysis into decisions regarding investments in transport infrastructure and changes in procedures for cross-border movement. Workshops could be used to inform transport professionals, shippers and consignees, and forwarders of the techniques used in supply-chain management.	2. Regional workshops could be used to share information among transport professionals, shippers and consignees, and forwarders to improve supply-chain logistics in the region. This would be particularly helpful for improving regional and international trade, particularly for landlocked regions.
3. Port reform and modernization for improved performance and logistics is a priority for development of the countries' trade in global markets. The measures would include: • Privatization of port management and operations, • Dedicated private terminal operations to expedite cargo handling, • Facilitating routing cargo through more efficient ports, and • Better coordination of movements between feeder and mainline vessels by improving port performance so the feeder vessels can operate on a fixed schedule.	3. Bilateral (and multilateral) dialogue and agreements can facilitate routing regional cargo through more efficient ports. For instance, routing cargo through more efficient ports on the western coast of the subcontinent could reduce travel time by about one week for exports to Europe.

National	Regional
4. Improve the physical design of land border crossings in high traffic crossings to reduce congestion and delays, with strategic investments in place of the current practice of ad hoc investments. Support private sector involvement in development of superstructure and operations at border crossings.	4. Coordination among relevant countries in effectively improving the physical design of strategic high-traffic land border crossings so that current congestion and delays are reduced dramatically.
5. Simplification of import and export cargo clearance procedures within the countries, including introduction of Automated Systems for Customs Data (or compatible) documentation.	5. Harmonization and standardization of cross-border cargo clearance procedures across countries.
6. Improved communication systems and adoption of automated technology for electronic transfer of information.	6. Compatibility of automated systems for effective electronic interchange of information.
7. Eliminate requirements for transshipment of cargo by trucks at border crossings and move toward increased transit access for vehicles from neighboring countries, so that multiple cargo handling and associated costs and delays are avoided. In addition, introduce: • Automatic weighing of vehicles at border points • Simplified procedures and risk-assessment strategies to replace current cargo inspection practices • Round-the-clock clearance of cargoes at high-density interchange points like Petrapole–Benapole and Gede–Darsana.	7. Revisions of bilateral transit protocols to facilitate uninterrupted movement of transit. Important changes include: • Replacement of the movement of transit cargo in truck convoys to flexible movement against specified time limits with in-bond goods; • The use of secure seals for rail cars or containers carrying transit cargo with very few or no inspections of cargo at the border, other than checking seals; • The Transports Internationaux Routiers (TIR) system for the carriage of goods approved by customs authorities from the transport of sealed containers using the TIR carnet; and • Common vehicle inspection and licensing procedures for trucks used to transport cargo across borders.
8. Monitoring/tracking systmes for cargo movement.	8. More effective mechanisms for monitoring the movement of the cargo, instead of the existing practice of using fixed routes and truck convoys. These could include: • Joint checking of cargoes at the origin and destination; • Electronic data interchange (EDI) between customs facilities within the country and across borders; • Identification numbers, bar codes, or other forms of electronic identification for trucks and cargo containers; • The use of a freight operation information system for real-time monitoring of trains, rail cars, and cargo; and • Tracking systems for transit cargo carried by trucks.

(Table continues on the following page.)

TABLE 6.1   (continued)

National	Regional
9. Assignment of liability for the carriage of goods within the country to encourage more efficient multimodal transport.	9. Assignment of liability for the carriage of goods and harmonization of this liability scheme across regional and international borders.
10. Development of full rake sidings for rail, night unloading facilities, and terminal facilities at major loading and unloading points.	
11. Development of night navigation facilities on selected inland waterways in Bangladesh and in the waterways linking Northeast India and West Bengal.	
12. For Bangladesh, a cohesive plan identifying key bridges that need upgrading along high-traffic corridors, taking into account ongoing efforts to strengthen bridges on the Dhaka-Chittagong highway.	

Medium and Long term

National	Regional
1. Investments in road network infrastructure, including widening roadways and constructing divided highways. Bangladesh would base this on a review and update of the existing road master plan. India would incorporate planned and ongoing road projects, including the Golden Quadrilateral and West Bengal north-south highway, and a medium-term plan for less congested road links to and among the Northeastern states.	1. Investments at border crossings to facilitate easier two-way flow of traffic.
2. Increased movement of containerized goods, particularly high-value commodities. It would be useful to review (a) the Container Corporation of India (CONCOR) experience and (b) the experience of Nepal ICDs, including efforts to integrate private sector operations and prepare recommendations for making the process more efficient, effective, and transparent.	2. Extend the movement of containerized goods, particularly high-value commodities such as yarn, across national and regional borders.
3. Strengthening and widening bridges where necessary, particularly along selected roadways for Bangladesh and Northeast India.	

National	Regional
4. The TTTCs could oversee a review of the progress and plans for harmonization of rail networks to determine the likely impact on national traffic flows. Other items on the rail agenda would include proposing standards for rolling stock, such as the configuration of container rail cars, the identification system for rail cars, and the introduction of air brakes and semi-automatic couplers for the freight cars crossing the border between India and Bangladesh. Finally the review committee would look at increased private sector involvement in unit train operations, especially proposals for shipping lines and other logistic providers to operate trains for the movement of containers inland.	4. A review of the progress and plans for harmonization of rail networks to determine the likely impact on regional traffic flows. The review should include ways to introduce, expand, and improve block train operations and rail-based ICDs to serve landlocked areas; scope for private sector operations.
5. Modern laws and regulations covering clearer assignment of liabilities for the carriage of cargo, permitting tighter integration of intermodal movements and reducing barriers to entry for potential third-party logistic providers.	5. Harmonization of laws and regulations in the region to enable clear assignment of liabilities for the carriage of cargo and permit tighter integration of intermodal movements across national and international borders. (There is considerable international experience and legal precedence concerning this issue.)

6. Expand e-commerce opportunities more broadly to remote sectors, industries, and regions so that small and medium enterprises can market their products directly to businesses and markets. This would involve:
  • Access to assured data communications and Internet services,
  • Supportive legislation to allow financial transactions over the Internet that are both secure and legally binding,
  • Increased privatization of telecommunications and Internet services,
  • Establishment of a public-private partnership to ensure a competitive environment for e-commerce services, and
  • Training for small- and medium-scale businesses for effective use and development of services.
	6. New systems are needed for improving voice and data transmissions between customs checkpoints at the border crossings and between the checkpoints and central customs offices and seaports. Initially this could be accomplished through a value-added network used by customs. This could be expanded to the ICDs and other border crossings that would act as a center of efficient and effective communications for scheduling and coordinating movements with other activities on the logistics chain. Ultimately, it should allow the users to input data electronically through multiple ports and, eventually, through the Internet.

7. In the long term, systematically introduce measures to move toward offering shippers door-to-door economical just-in-time delivery service, which is important for the country to gain position in the global market.	7. In the long term, systematically introduce measures to move toward offering shippers door-to-door economical just-in-time delivery service, which is important for the region to gain position in the global market.
	8. Implementation of a smart card system for expediting all the transactions associated with cross-border movements.

the need for such a forum that is not necessarily a permanent institution, but rather a flexible adaptable body that can bring together issues and suggest options for various stakeholders from the relevant countries, including the private and public sectors.

The subregion covered by this report has made a beginning in establishing regional dialogue. Under SAARC, a subregional grouping with representation from the four relevant countries (Bangladesh, Bhutan, India, and Nepal) has already been established. The private sector in the subregion (led by the chambers of commerce) has signed a memorandum of understanding. It has launched the Emerging East Initiative to promote investment and trade in the subregion. The private sector is in the process of formalizing the institution. To address cross–sectoral issues on transport, trade facilitation, and logistics, and to support continual private and public sector inputs, technical committees (Transport and Trade Facilitation Technical Committees or TTTCs) were formed in Bangladesh, Bhutan, and Nepal, after our national consultative workshops in July 1999. These committees consist of key governmental representatives from the ministries of commerce, transport, customs, and other agencies, and private sector representatives from the chambers of commerce, freight forwarders' associations, shippers' councils, and other organizations.

There is need for a regional public-private forum to identify methods for improving logistics for both intraregional and extraregional trade, set priorities and short-term targets to achieve the greatest benefits, and develop a forceful and sustainable program for improving logistics in the region. This forum or regional technical committee would have a tripartite representation:

- Government representatives from the relevant trade, transport, and customs agencies to provide the policy and public infrastructure perspective;

- Private sector representatives of the shippers, consignees, chambers of commerce, and logistics providers to provide a private sector and commercial perspective; and

- Specialists from international organizations, academia, and consulting organizations with detailed knowledge of trade facilitation, supply chain management, and logistics services to provide information on best practices, as well as on practical limitations of reforms experienced in other regional trade blocs.

The institutional form, mandate, and terms of reference of the regional technical committee would be examined in consultation with regional stakeholders as part of a process of discussing the findings of this report at national workshops and a regional conference. This chapter will present preliminary ideas for the range and scope of tasks that the regional technical committee would address. The committee would review ongoing efforts in the region and elsewhere and develop a time-bound action plan. The committee would coordinate with SAARC and the subregional quadrangle body, the private sector's Emerging East Initiative group, the national TTTCs, and other relevant public and private agencies mentioned earlier. The implementation of its recommendations would require domestic and bilateral initiatives and would be the responsibility of the TTTCs in each country.

PRELIMINARY AGENDA

It is important to point out that, in addition to several issues that require regional approaches and bilateral or multilateral agreements, there are some areas that can be more efficiently dealt with at a national level. There are three agendas to be addressed:

- Coordination of transport sector reform and investment, which would be addressed at a national level through the individual TTTCs,

- Trade facilitation, which would be addressed at a regional level through the regional technical committee, and

- The development of business-to-business e-commerce at both the national and local levels.

There would be need for both short- and long term improvements. The short-term improvements would address problems related to:

- The exchange of goods between East and Northeast India;

- Bhutan and Nepal trade with international markets and with regional markets (in the case of the latter, many commodities have short shelf lives); and

- The trade between Bangladesh and neighboring countries, including Northeastern Indian states, and strategic improvements for Bangladesh transport and logistics systems to improve global trade.

These would also have significant implications for improved logistics in the individual countries. The long-term improvements would focus on the region's capacity to meet the logistics requirements for trade in high-value goods.

Coordination of Transport Sector Reform and Investment

The key areas for attention would be the development or improvement of seaport and landport facilities to serve the foreign trade of all countries, including the landlocked ones; the coordination of the investment and maintenance of the transport linkages across borders; and the introduction of modern technology for monitoring the flow of cargo and vehicles across borders.

A priority area for attention that has direct implications for opportunities in the global markets

for the countries is the improvement of seaports. Efforts to reform the port sectors in India and Bangladesh are longstanding but have achieved relatively little, other than the recent private sector initiatives on the west coast of India and the private sector Patenga port that is being planned in Bangladesh. In contrast, East Asia has achieved rapid gains in port productivity and generated substantial investment in port infrastructure and equipment over the last three decades. The port sector has been rationalized, customs procedures have been automated, and the private sector has taken over operations of several ports. Although container traffic volumes have increased in South Asia, the time and costs for transferring containers has not declined substantially. Calcutta and Chittagong remain the most inefficient components of the logistics chain, with average vessel waiting times of several days and container handling rates of less than six boxes per hour per handling point.

Port reform is crucial for improved logistics. It is the subject of several ongoing efforts at port modernization. A key element is private terminal operations, which would expedite cargo handling. For foreign shipments, improvements in the logistics associated with port handling and ocean transport is critical because of the dominance of the costs and the time associated with port handling and ocean transport. A reduction in the time for ocean transport would have a marked impact on total travel time. This can be accomplished in two ways: by routing cargo through more efficient ports and by coordinating movements between feeder and mainline vessels. The first will become more attractive as the rail container movements to the Indian ports on the western coast improve. The second requires improvements in port performance in order for the feeder vessels to operate on a fixed schedule. This involves the establishment of dedicated privately operated terminals. The first approach will reduce travel time by about one week for movements to

Europe. The second approach will reduce travel time by about three to five days.

The road, rail, and inland water transport networks require substantial improvements. The current networks have low average travel speeds, limited hours of operation, and relatively high losses due to poor maintenance. Investment needs in network infrastructure include widening roadways, constructing dual carriageway roads, strengthening bridges, deepening and straightening navigational channels, harmonizing rail lines, double tracking high-density rail corridors, developing better rail terminals, standardizing rail car technology, installing systems to more closely monitor the movements of rolling stock, and providing better signaling systems. Improvements in operation should include providing larger-capacity, more powerful, and more reliable transport units, introducing private sector management; and making greater use of telecommunications and electronic data processing. All of these require careful study and planning at this stage if they are to be effectively implemented during this decade.

The physical design of the cross-border facilities needs to be dramatically improved. The services provided at these facilities will depend on the volume of cargo handled, as well as on the transport modes being served and the protocol governing the cross-border movements. Basic operational analysis should be applied to the capacity of processing gates, parking areas, and intermediate storage areas to determine the amount of investment required to avoid congestion and limit delays. Benapole is an example of ad hoc planning where there have been significant investments, but the investments were not well planned to fill gaps and inadequacies directed at the right components. As a result, the various components of the facility do not work well together. Many of the other border crossings have little or no investment, and transport is delayed waiting for service to be brought to the site. One of the advantages of creating a limited number of border crossings is that investment can be concentrated and traffic levels will be sufficient to encourage private logistics service providers to locate offices there. Where possible, the private sector should finance the development of the superstructure at the border crossing.

Rail reform is important for the movement of goods over long distances and in areas not well served by the road network. At a national as well as a regional level, there would be a need to review the progress and plans for harmonization of rail networks to determine the likely impact on national and regional traffic flows. At the national level, the TTTC would be responsible for the review process, whereas at the regional level a regional committee would oversee the review process. The review should include ways to introduce, expand, and improve block train operations and rail-based ICDs to serve landlocked areas. There would be need to review the experience of Nepalese ICDs, including efforts to provide private sector operations and prepare recommendations for making the process more efficient, effective, and transparent. Other items on the agenda would include proposing standards for rolling stock, including the configuration of container wagons, the identification system for wagons, and the introduction of air brakes and semiautomatic couplers for the freight wagons crossing the border between India and Bangladesh. Finally the review committee would look at increased private sector involvement in unit train operations, especially proposals for shipping lines and other logistics providers to operate trains for the movement of containers inland.

Even as efforts are underway to undo the restrictive trade practices of earlier decades, it is important to look ahead to the fundamental ways in which trade is changing and to develop strategies for creating or at least maintaining a competitive advantage. Two areas in which the region must catch up with the rest of the world are multimodal transport and the assignment of liability for carriage of goods. Although the freight transport in all four countries can accommodate intermodal movements, the operations of the individual modal services are not integrated. Despite the introduction of the multimodal transport act in India, there has been relatively little success in offering to shippers and consignees a door-to-door service that is both efficient and economical.

One of the constraints limiting multimodal transport is the lack of modern laws and regulations covering the assignment of liabilities for carriage of cargo. Clearer assignment of liabilities permits tighter integration of intermodal movements and reduces the barriers to entry for potential third-party logistic providers. It also makes railroads and trucking companies improve their quality of service to limit their exposure due to loss or damage of cargo. There is a considerable body of international experience and legal precedence in this issue. There is little reason for delaying the enactment of these laws and regulations.

Regional Trade Facilitation

The second agenda, regional trade facilitation, would cover protocols and procedures. In particular it would focus on the need for:

- Simplification and standardization of cross-border cargo clearance procedures, and

- Revision of bilateral transit protocols.

The cost and time for customs procedures at the land borders have been reduced through ongoing national efforts to reform customs procedures.

These include the simplification of documents, introduction of ASYCUDA documentation, and adoption of new technologies, including the electronic transfer of information using electronic data interchange for administration, commerce, and transport protocol. These reforms need to be applied more consistently at the seaports and border crossings across the region. The standardization and simplification of documents should be coordinated so that the same documents are used on both sides of a border. The procedures should be simplified to increase institutional efficiency and to reduce both formal and informal costs.

Improvements in communications and document transfer are required so that the agencies involved in monitoring border crossings are informed of upcoming movements and have the supporting documentation readily accessible, preferably in electronic form. Efficient exchange of information between shippers and customs officers, and shippers and shipping lines, as well as between the customs officers on both sides of a border crossing, can significantly reduce the time required for cargo movements as well as the uncertainty associated with these movements. This will be especially important for efficient operation of the ICDs at the Nepalese border, the major border crossings between India and Bangladesh, and the seaports handling imports, exports, and transit cargoes.

The existing bilateral transit protocols are a work in progress. They have been useful in opening borders that had been closed and creating opportunities for transit cargo to move from landlocked areas. They have not, however, provided efficient mechanisms for handling transit cargo, but treat them instead like import or export cargo. The first priority is to end the remaining prohibitions on cross-border movements of cargo for both regional and international trade. The next is to eliminate the remaining requirements for transshipment of cargo between the vehicles at the border. After that, it will be necessary to introduce the various procedures used in different trading blocs for the efficient movement of transit cargo.

The elimination of transshipments for road transport is important because the cost and time for transport increases dramatically where cargo must be transferred between the trucks of each country.[2] The shipper incurs the additional cost for multiple handlings and is prevented from using the less costly of the two transport providers for the entire trip. This system limits the potential for backhaul cargoes, thereby increasing the cost of transport. New bilateral transit protocols should allow uninterrupted movement of transit goods in-bond. In particular, the protocols with Bangladesh need to be modified to allow trucks from other countries to operate in Bangladesh. This will not only improve Bangladesh's trade with its neighbors, but it would also attract transit traffic to use the logistics services in Bangladesh.

Some of the more important customs reforms that need to be introduced to facilitate cross-border movement of transit traffic, as well as reforms related to bilateral trade, include:

- Replacement of the movement of transit cargo in truck convoys to flexible movement against specified time limits.

- The use of secure seals for wagons or containers carrying transit cargo, along with the practice of conducting very few or no inspections of cargo at the border, other than checking the seals.

---

2. The railways and the inland waterways transportation networks already have protocols for the movement of vehicles and vessels across borders.

- Common vehicle inspections and licensing procedures for trucks used to transport cargo across borders.

- Automatic weighing of vehicles at border points.

- The TIR system for the carriage of goods approved by customs authorities from the transport of sealed containers using the TIR carnet.

- Simple procedures and risk-assessment strategies to replace current cargo inspection practices.

- Round-the-clock clearance of cargoes at high-density interchange points such as Petrapole-Benapole and Gede/Darsana.

- Development of full rake sidings, night unloading facilities, and terminal facilities at major loading and unloading points.

These reforms should be accomplished over the next three years. The regional technical committee would examine methods for expediting their implementation.

There is a need to modify the protocols to offer more routes and improve border crossings. It is important to identify specific border crossings where government officials intend to provide significant infrastructure and a larger customs presence. These crossings will handle a majority of the movements by road and rail. It is also important to identify minor border crossings that will have a lower level of service but will provide an outlet for areas that have relatively low volumes of trade and are far from the major crossings. The selection of routes is a more contentious issue. Any limitation on routes will create inefficiencies. The goal should be to give shippers free access to the transport network while still keeping them accountable for safely moving cargo to its destination. Under this system, the market would decide the most effective route, depending on the type of commodity and the final destination.

The mechanism for monitoring the movement of the cargo would have to be more sophisticated than the use of fixed routes and truck convoys. A variety of ways to accomplish this were mentioned in the previous paragraph. Other innovations that could be introduced include:

- Joint checking of cargoes at the origin and destination;

- EDI between customs facilities within the country and across borders;

- Identification numbers, bar codes, or other forms of electronic identification for trucks and cargo containers;

- The use of freight operation information system for real-time monitoring of trains, wagons, and cargo; and

- Tracking systems for transit cargo carried by trucks.

The committee should evaluate the alternatives and select those that can be implemented in the next five years. The committee would also look at the longer-term implementation of a smart card system for expediting all the transactions associated with cross-border movements.

The committee would examine current regulations of the logistics industry and identify ways to foster greater competition while at the same time allowing for vertical integration through the introduction of full-service, third-party logistics providers. Logistics services were traditionally provided by a number of different actors, each providing a specific service. In the 1970s, with the advent of multimodal transportation, shipping lines and freight forwarders sought to provide door-to-door movement of cargoes. However, existing regulations slowed the integration of transport services and protected the less efficient providers of individual logistics services. Nevertheless, consolidation did occur. The same companies now provide customs clearance and forwarding. Forwarding agents are able to contract directly with transport companies and form alliances with foreign forwarding agents to provide door-to-door services. Forwarders also sought to provide cargo consolidation. However, the ports are reluctant to give up this role, and they frequently require shippers and consignees to consolidate or deconsolidate their cargo within the port boundaries.

Modern integrated logistics service providers offer a full range of logistics services, including intermediate storage, consolidation, packaging, inventory control, customs clearance, and cargo tracking, as well as arranging for basic transport services. In some cases, they will also take responsibility for the inventories and sales of the cargoes. The development of these integrated services has yet to occur in South Asia. Third-party logistics will become more important, both as trade in high-value goods increases and as producers focus on their competitive advantage in research, production, and marketing, and rely on others to provide efficient logistics functions. For low-value goods, it will continue to be more efficient to negotiate individual services between the shippers and suppliers of the services.

Development of Business-to-Business e-Commerce

The third agenda would be the development of better trade communications. The rapid evolution of telecommunications services and the importance of those services to trade extends from creating more efficiency on the major trade routes to providing service to the more remote, less-developed areas. The unprecedented accessibility provided by the Internet is matched by the scalability of its services. The first phase of electronic commerce was limited to proprietary systems developed by major transport companies and trading organizations. The second phase utilized value-added networks that provided EDI services developed by customs organizations, seaports, and other government agencies. The third phase is the ongoing development of Internet-based business-to-business transactions using Extensible Markup Language (XML) messaging. It is this latter system that offers the greatest opportunities for improvements in trade and logistics in areas located away from the major trade routes. These systems facilitate communication and coordination between importers/exporters and foreign markets, and between shippers and customs. It also creates opportunities for more efficient use of the available transport services. This can lead to a reduction in both the cost and time for transport of goods.

EDI and business-to-business e-commerce are two areas of increasing importance. Immediate attention should be given to implementing EDI services that are accessible to both regional customs authorities and logistics providers involved in regional trade.

Business-to-business e-commerce is a rapidly expanding area of trade that makes use of modern communications technologies to broaden the market in which buyers and sellers conduct business and to reduce the costs of the transactions in this market. This method of trade began with large companies that established proprietary communications and data management networks to facilitate the interaction between their production units and suppliers. In recent years, this effort has been expanded to external networks that accommodate bidding by multiple suppliers

against specifications and terms of tendering posted by buyers. Most recently, this has expanded into Web hosting of auction sites on the Internet. Within a few years, it is anticipated that this innovation, combined with simplified Web hosting and improved Web browsers, will allow small- and medium-scale enterprises to market their products directly to customers or, more importantly, to businesses through the Internet. If these enterprises are to succeed in this market, they will require access to good-quality data communications and Internet services. They will also require supporting legislation to allow financial transactions over the Internet that are both secure and legally binding.

Efforts to expand e-commerce have generally begun with the private sector, followed by academic and government attempts to provide broader access to this way of doing business. A private-public partnership should be established to ensure that a competitive environment is developed for providing e-commerce services and that publicly supported training and promotional efforts focus on small and medium businesses. Among the strategic partners to be included in this effort are the telecommunications companies, chambers of commerce, and industrial federations. Their focus would be to provide telecommunications access and Internet services for businesses at a reasonable cost, as well as providing training in the use of e-commerce and technical assistance for the creation of Web sites and Internet markets.

The potential to improve information services is constrained by two factors. The first is the quality and coverage of telecommunications services in the remote areas of the region. The second is the lack of private sector participation in the provision of these services, especially the Internet. Government regulation of Internet service providers prevents competition, thereby maintaining relatively high prices and low quality of service. It also raises questions about the security of transmitted messages.

New systems are needed for improving voice and data transmission between customs checkpoints at the border crossings and between the checkpoints and central customs offices and seaports. Initially this could be accomplished through a value-added network used by customs. This could be expanded to the ICDs and other border crossings, which would act as a center of efficient and effective communications for scheduling and coordinating movements with other activities on the logistics chain. Ultimately, it should allow the users to input data electronically through multiple ports and eventually through the Internet.

REGIONAL CAPACITY BUILDING

As mentioned earlier, regional stakeholders will develop the exact structure of the regional committee, as well as its mode of working, coordination with existing regional and national entities involved in transport and logistics, and the participation of international agencies. It would be developed as a follow-up to this study and to subsequent discussions with these stakeholders in national workshops and a regional conference.

A separate effort is needed to develop the capacity within the public and private sectors to perform supply chain analysis. One of the difficulties in reaching agreements on how to improve the efficiency of the shipment of goods within and beyond a region is that the discussion between the public and private sectors rarely rises above the level of anecdotes. Occasionally a detailed analysis will be performed of one component of the supply chain. Supply chain analysis allows public officials, shippers, consignees, and logistics providers to identify major bottlenecks and other inefficiencies in trade logistics and to assess the costs and benefits of initiatives to improve the performance of individual components of the supply chain. The analysis presented in this report suggests that improvements in seaports will offer the greatest return on investment followed by improvements in the cross-border procedures. However, these findings apply to specific combinations of cargoes and routes. The same type of analysis needs to be performed as part of any effort to increase the efficiency of trade for a specific commodity and origin/destination pair.

Technical assistance should be provided to assist transport and planning ministries, development banks, freight forwarders, major shippers, and experts in logistics in the techniques of supply chain analysis. Procedures should be developed for incorporating supply chain analysis into decisions regarding both investments in transport infrastructure and changes in procedures for cross-border movements. Workshops could be used to inform transport professions, shippers and consignees, and forwarders about the techniques used in supply chain management.

Bibliography

BACKGROUND NOTES

Background Note 1: Private Sector Consultative Meeting, *Summary Proceedings of the Meeting*, Kathmandu, February 1999. South Asia Regional Initiative on Transport.

Background Note 2: Trucking Sector: A Note. prepared by Peter H.Yee (consultant), 2000

Background Note 3: Brief Report on Bangladesh Railway. prepared by M. R. Prakash (consultant), 2000

Background Note 4: Container Trade in Bangladesh—An Overview. prepared by M.R.Parkash, 2000

Background Note 5: Characteristics of Inland Waterway Transport—prepared by S.M. Matin (consultant), 2000

Background Note 6: Bangladesh Transport Corridor Study, prepared by S.M.Matin, 1998

Background Note 7: Analysis of Phulbari Corridor. prepared by the Nepal Center for Contemporary Studies, Kathmandu. 1999

Background Note 8: Cross Border Procedures: A Note, prepared by Peter H. Yee

Background Note 9: Impediments to Efficient Cross Border Procedures in South Asia, prepared by Peter H.Yee

Background Note 10: "Private Sector Initiatives in Transport in South Asia: A Note" prepared by Peter H. Yee, 1999.

Background Note 11:. Working Group Meeting Kathmandu February 4, 1999. South Asia Regional Transport and Facilitation Initiative, The World Bank. Prepared by S. M. Matin.

Background Note 12: Bangladesh's Transshipment Proposal: Issues Brief, prepared by Uma Subramanian, World Bank, September 1999.

Background Note 13: "Strengthening Bhutan's Development Cooperation in the South Asia Sub-region" prepared by Chado Tshering (summer intern), 1998.

Background Note 14: "Bhutan: Trade and Industries Sector"—prepared by Chado Tshering, 1998.

OTHER REFERENCES

Agarwal, Om, 1998. "South Asia: An Overview of Trade Facilitation and Transport," Draft Consultant Report, prepared for the World Bank.

Amjadi, A., and L. Alan Winters. 1997. "Transport Costs and "Natural Integration in Mercosur." Policy Research Working Paper 1742. World Bank, Washington, D.C.

Bandara, J. S., and M. McGillivray. 1998. "Trade Policy Reforms in South Asia." London: Blackwell.

Blomstrom, Magnus and Ari Kokko 1997. "Regional Integration and Foreign direct Investment—A conceptual Framework and Three Cases" The World Bank, Policy Research Working paper 1750. Washington D.C.

Bougheas, Spiros, P.O. Demetrades, and E.L.W. Morgenroth. 1999. "Infrastructure, Costs and Trade." *Journal of Development Economics* 47.

Carl, Hans. 1999. Harmonization of the Transport Law of Bangladesh, Bhutan, India and Nepal, Manuscript, United Nations Center for Trade and Development.

Centre for Policy Research and Centre for Policy Dialogue, 1995. "Indo-Bangladesh Dialogue, Economic and Trade Cooperation" Published by the Center for Policy Research, New Delhi.

CII-FNCCI, 1995. Report on Indo-Nepal Joint Economic Cooperation" prepared by the CII-FNCCI Joint Task Force.

Datt, Gaurav and Martin Ravallion, 1990. "Regional Disparities, Targeting, and Poverty in India" The World Bank, Working Papers 375.

Datt, Gaurav and Martin Ravallion, 1996 "Why Have Some Indian States Done Better Than Others at Reducing Rural Poverty?" The World Bank Policy Research Working Paper 1594, Washington D.C.

de Castro, C.F. 1994. "Nepal, Multimodal Transit and Trade Facilitation Project, Facilitation Component, Note for Project Preparation". Prepared for the World Bank, Washington D.C.

de Monie, G. 1995."Multimodal Transit and Trade Facilitation Project" The World Bank. Washington D.C.

Ghei, Rita S. 1993. "Bangladesh Transport & Trade Logistics Study". Draft Report. Prepared for the World Bank, Washington D.C.

Government of Nagaland, 1994. "Feasibility Study for Upgrading of state Highway Kohima-Wokha-Mokochung Amguri" Government of Nagaland, Public Works Department (Roads & Bridges), Consulting Engineering Services (India) Private Limited.

Government of West Bengal 1996. "Strategic Options Study for State Roads Projects in West Bengal, Final Report". Government of West Bengal, Public Works (roads) Department.

Halcrow & Partners, 1999. "North-South Corridor Development Project in West Bengal" Inception Report by Sir William Halcrow & Partners Limited. Prepared for the Asian Development Bank.

Hossain, M., I. Islam, R. Kibria. 1998. *The South Asian Economies: Transformation, Opportunities, and Challenges*. London: Routledge.

IMF (International Monetary Fund). 1999a. *Direction of Trade Statistics*. Washington, D.C.

———. 1999b. *International Financial Statistics Yearbook*. Washington, D.C.

Jonathan Stevens and Peter Cook, 1999 "South Asia Sub-Regional Transport Corridor Study" draft final consultant report, prepared for the World Bank.

Lakshmanan, T. R., and William P. Anderson. 1999. "Trade and Transport Integration: Lessons from the North American Experience." Paper presented at the World Bank/ESCAP Regional Technical Workshop on Transport and Transit Facilitation, Bangkok. April 1999.

Lakshmanan, T. R., Uma Subramanian, William P. Anderson, and Frannie A. Léautier, 2001. *Integration of Transport and Trade Facilitation: Selected Regional Case Studies.* The World Bank. Washington D.C.

Leautier, Frannie A. 1999. "Transport in South Asia: Issues and Options." Paper presented at the World Bank/ESCAP Regional Technical Workshop on Transport and Transit Facilitation, Bangkok. April 1999.

Maxwell, T. 1999. "Impediments to Exporting." Paper presented at the World Bank/ESCAP Regional Technical Workshop on Transport and Transit Facilitation, Bangkok. April 1999.

Meghalaya Economic Development Council, 1997. "A Meghalaya Economic Development Council Approach Paper on Identification of Existing Infrastructural Gaps in Core Sectors and Restructuring Same in Consonance with the Economic Policy of the State of Meghalaya" Working Group on behalf of Chairman, Meghalaya Economic Development Council.

National Council of Applied Economic Research, 1994. "Cross-Border Trade Between India and Bangladesh" (Draft). Study for the World Bank.

Panagariya, Arvind, Shekhar Shah and Deepak Mishra, 1996. Demand Elasticities in International Trade: Are they Really Low? Policy Research Working Paper 1712, The World Bank, Washington D.C.

Paul-Majumder, Pratima and Anwara Begum, 2000. The Gender Imbalances in the Export Oriented Garment Industry in Bangladesh. Working Paper Series No.12. Policy Research Report on Gender and Development. The World Bank.

Peters, Hans J. 1990 "India's Growing Conflict between Trade and Transport, Issues and Options", The World Bank, Working Papers Working Paper Series-346.

Peters, Hans J. 1993. *The Maritime Transport Crisis.* World Bank Discussion Paper 220. Washington, D.C.

Pigato, M., et al. 1997. *South Asia's Integration into the World Economy.* The World Bank, Washington, D.C.

Pitigala, Nihal, 2000. Trade Agreements in the South Asia Region: Background and Introduction. Draft Note for Discussion. The World Bank, Washington, D.C.

Rahman, Mustafizur. 1996. "Regional Trade Co-operation in the SAARC: Issues of Transition from SAPTA to SAFTA." Paper presented at the regional seminar on the South Asia Free Trade Area organized by the SAARC Chamber of Commerce in Dhaka, December 17, 1996.

Ravallion, Martin 1991 "The Challenging Arithmetic of Poverty in Bangladesh" The World Bank, Working Paper 586, Washington D.C..

Rao, V.L., Srinath Baruah and R. Upendra Das, 1996. "India's Border Trade with Select Neighbouring Countries" (Draft), Research Information System for the Non-Aligned and Other Developing Countries, New Delhi.

South Asian Association for Regional Cooperation 1999. "Third Meeting of SAARC Commerce Ministers in Dhaka, Report". SAARC, Kathmandu.

Sowinski, Lara L. 2000. "Is There a Perfect Logistics Product in the Market?" *World Trade* (February).

Subramanian, Uma, 1999. "South Asia Transport: Issues and Options." Paper presented at the World Bank /ESCAP Regional Technical Workshop on Transport and Transit Facilitation, Bangkok. April 1999.

World Bank. 1994. *World Development Report.* New York: Oxford University Press.

———. 1994 "India Container Transport Logistics Project" Staff Appraisal Report, The World Bank, May 1994.

———. 1995 "Improving African Transport Corridors." Operations Evaluation Department, Precis Number 84. Washington, D.C.

———. 1995 "India Transport Sector: Long Term Issues" Report No. 13192-IN. Washington D.C.

———. 1996 "China Container Transport Services and Trade: Framework for an Efficient Container Transport System" Report No. 15303-CHA. Washington D.C.

———. 1996. "Bangladesh, Trade Policy Reform for Higher Export Growth". (Draft confidential Report No. 15900-BD). Washington D.C.

———. 1996. "Industrializing Bangladesh through Exports and Jobs—a strategy for one generation—volume II." Washington D.C.

———. 1999a. Proceedings of the Regional Technical Workshop on Transport and Transit Facilitation, World Bank/UN ESCAP sponsored workshop for South Asian delegates in Bangkok, April, 1999. (World Bank website: http://www.worldbank.org/html/fpd/transport/publicat/twu-34.pdf)

———. 1999b. Regional Technical Workshop on Transport and Transit Facilitation, Bangkok (Papers and Presentations).

———. 1999c. *World Development Indicators.* Washington D.C.

———. 1999d. "Bangladesh: Key Challenges for the Next Millennium" Washington D.C.

———. 1999e. "Bangladesh Trade Liberalization, its Pace and Impacts" Report No. 19591-BD. Washington D.C.

———. 2000a. *World Development Indicators.* Washington D.C.

———. 2000b. *Entering the Twenty-first Century: World Development Report 1999–2000.* New York: Oxford University Press.

Verghese, B. G. 1996. *India Northeast Resurgent: Ethnicity, Insurgency, Governance, Development.* Center for Policy Research. New Delhi: Konark Publishers.

Wodon, Quentin T. 1996. "A Profile of Poverty in Bangladesh: 1083–1992" The World Bank, South Asia Region, Internal Discussion Paper.

Maps

South Asia Intermodal Transportation Network

This section contains maps prepared for the logistics cost computer model mentioned in the text.

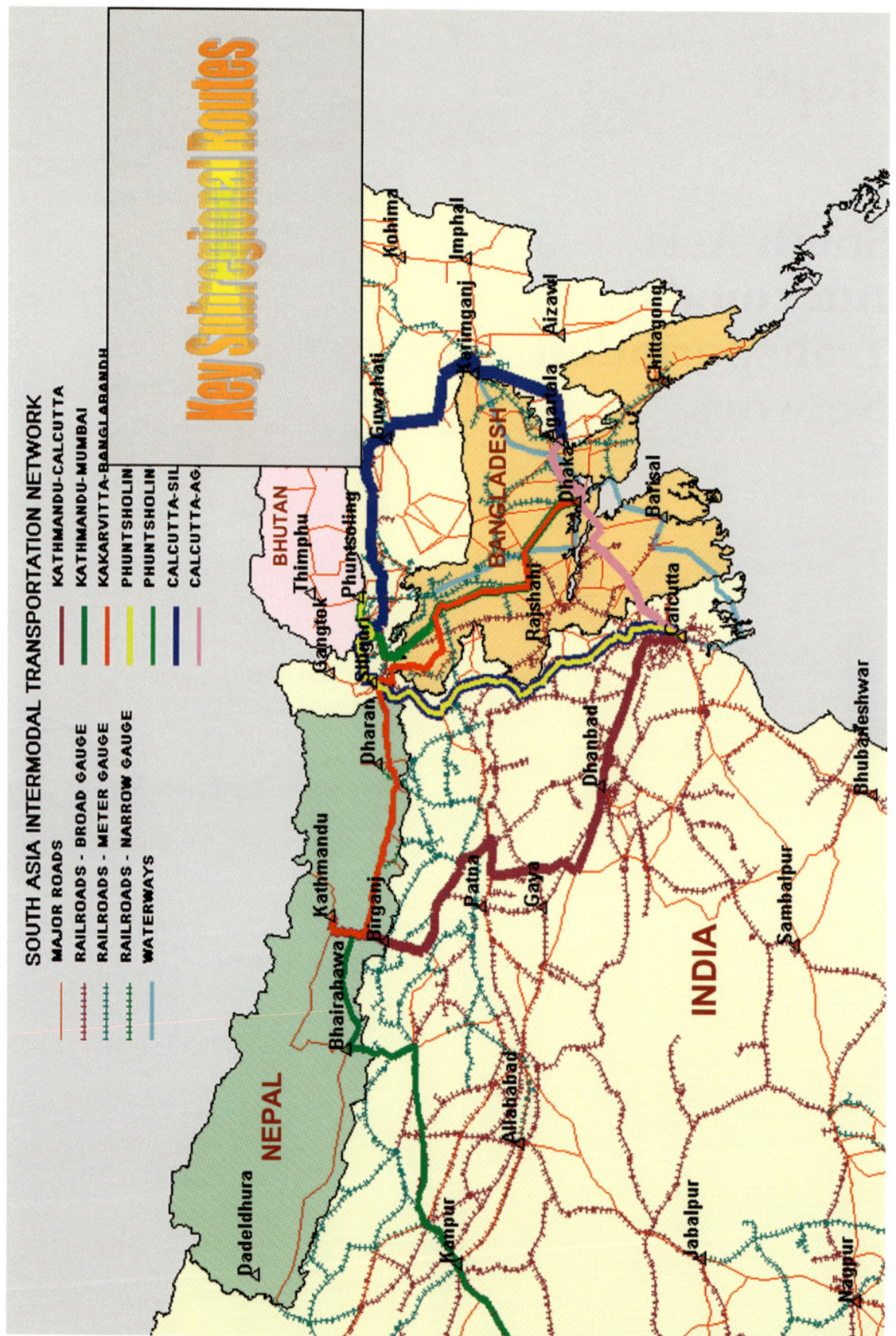

MAP 1

Key Subregional Routes

SOUTH ASIA INTERMODAL TRANSPORTATION NETWORK

MAJOR ROADS

RAILROADS - BROAD GAUGE

RAILROADS - METER GAUGE

RAILROADS - NARROW GAUGE

WATERWAYS

KATHMANDU-CALCUTTA

KATHMANDU-MUMBAI

KAKARVITTA-BANGLABANDH

PHUNTSHOLIN

PHUNTSHOLIN

CALCUTTA-SIL

CALCUTTA-AG

NEPAL

BHUTAN

BANGLADESH

INDIA

Dadeldhura

Bhairahawa

Kathmandu

Birganj

Kanpur

Allahabad

Jabalpur

Nagpur

Sambalpur

Bhubaneshwar

Gaya

Patna

Dhanbad

Calcutta

Barisal

Dhaka

Rajshahi

Agartala

Chittagong

Aizawl

Imphal

Kohima

Karimganj

Guwahati

Phuntsholing

Thimphu

Gangtok

Siliguri

Dharan

MAP 2

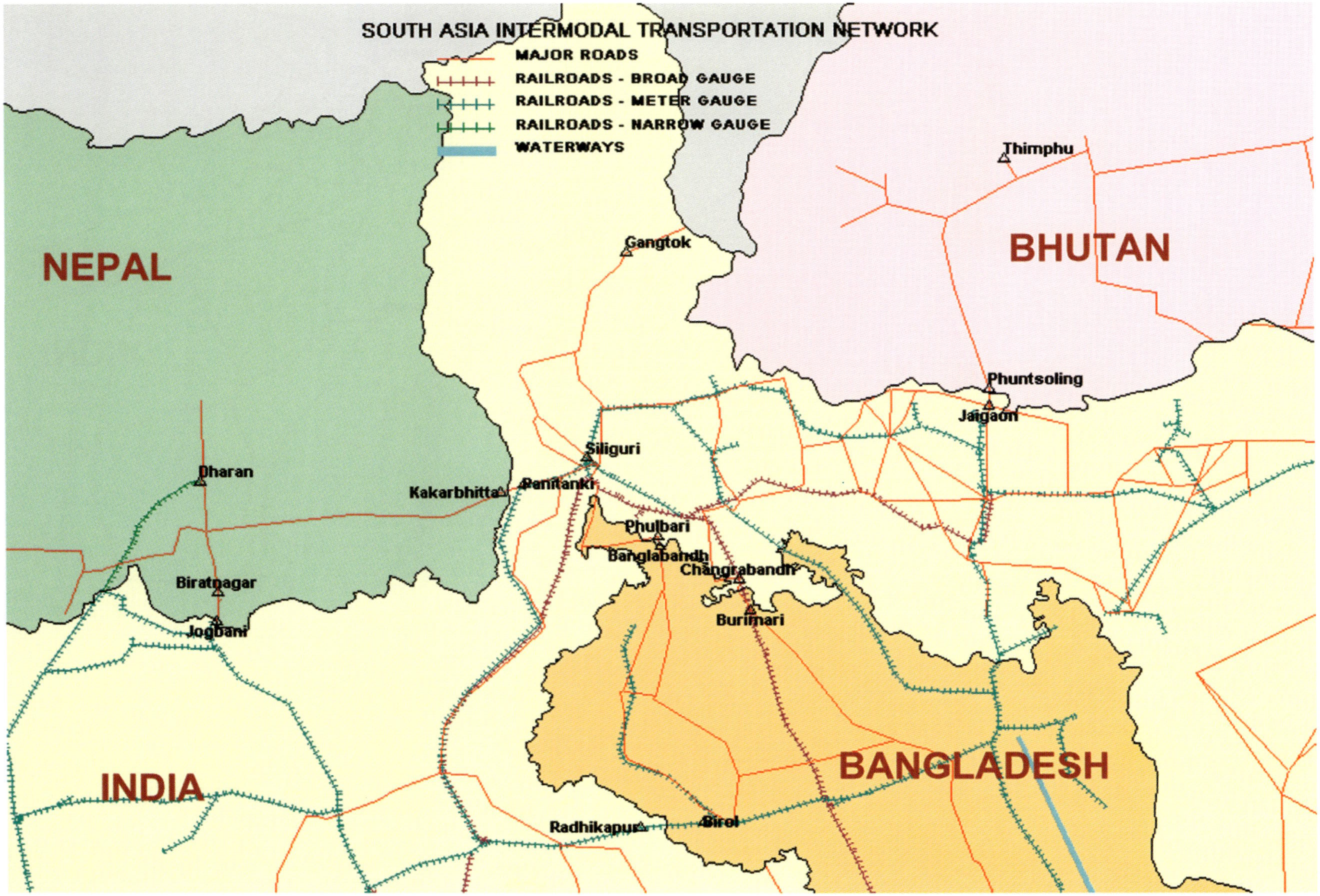

SOUTH ASIA INTERMODAL TRANSPORTATION NETWORK

MAJOR ROADS
RAILROADS - BROAD GAUGE
RAILROADS - METER GAUGE
RAILROADS - NARROW GAUGE
WATERWAYS

BHUTAN

Thimphu

Phuntsoling

Jaigaon

BANGLADESH

Gangtok

Burimari

Changrabandh

Banglabandh

Phulbari

Birol

Siliguri

Radhikapur

Panitanki

NEPAL

Kakarbhitta

Dharan

Biratnagar

Jogbani

INDIA

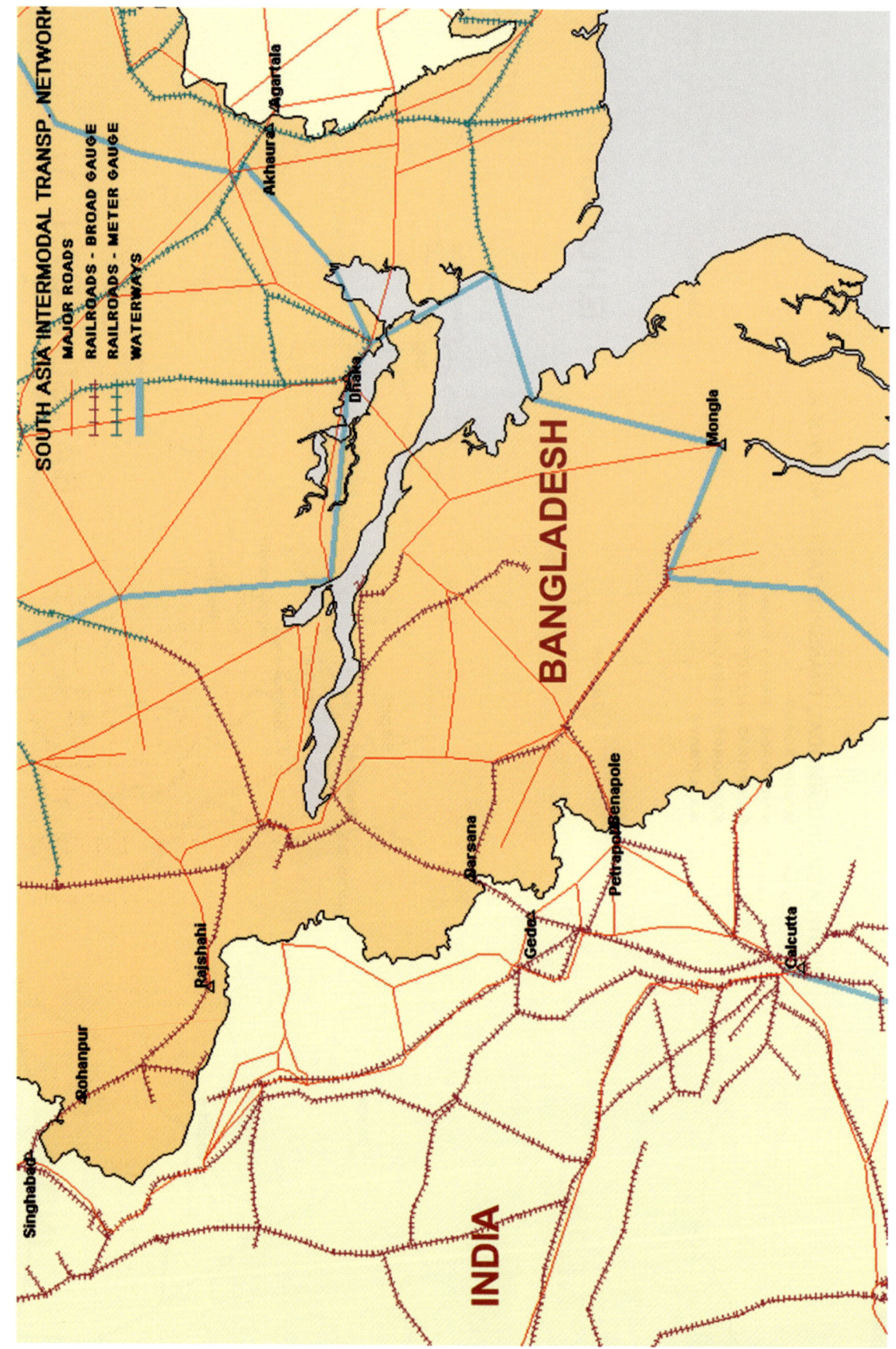

SOUTH ASIA INTERMODAL TRANSP. NETWORK

MAJOR ROADS
RAILROADS - BROAD GAUGE
RAILROADS - METER GAUGE
WATERWAYS

Singhabad
Rohanpur
Rajshahi
Akhaura
Agartala
Dhaka
Mongla
BANGLADESH
Darsana
Gede
Petrapole
Benapole
Calcutta
INDIA

MAP 3

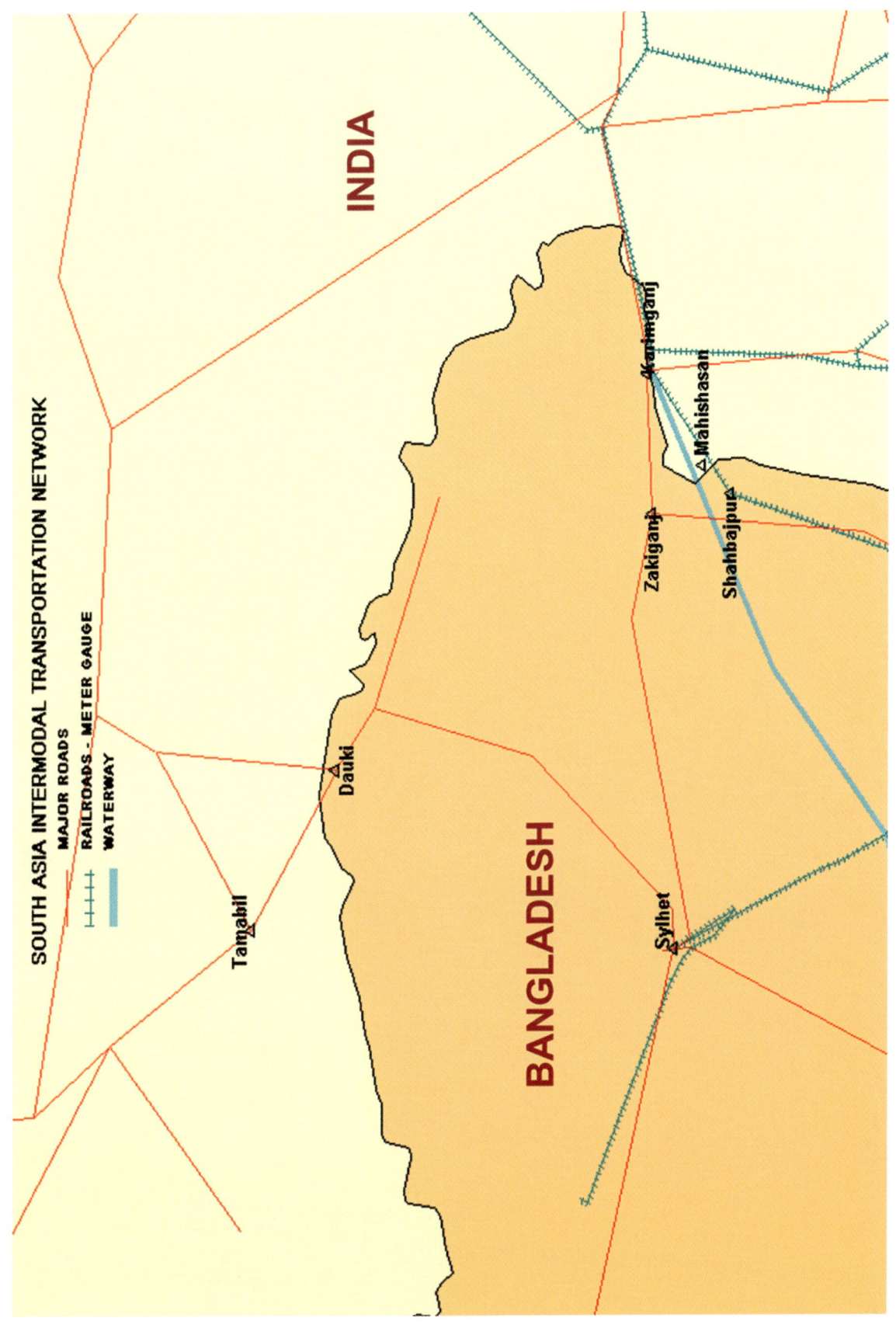

SOUTH ASIA INTERMODAL TRANSPORTATION NETWORK

MAJOR ROADS
RAILROADS - METER GAUGE
WATERWAY

INDIA

BANGLADESH

Tamabil

Dauki

Sylhet

Zakiganj

Shahbajpur

Karimganj

Mahishasan

MAP 4

125

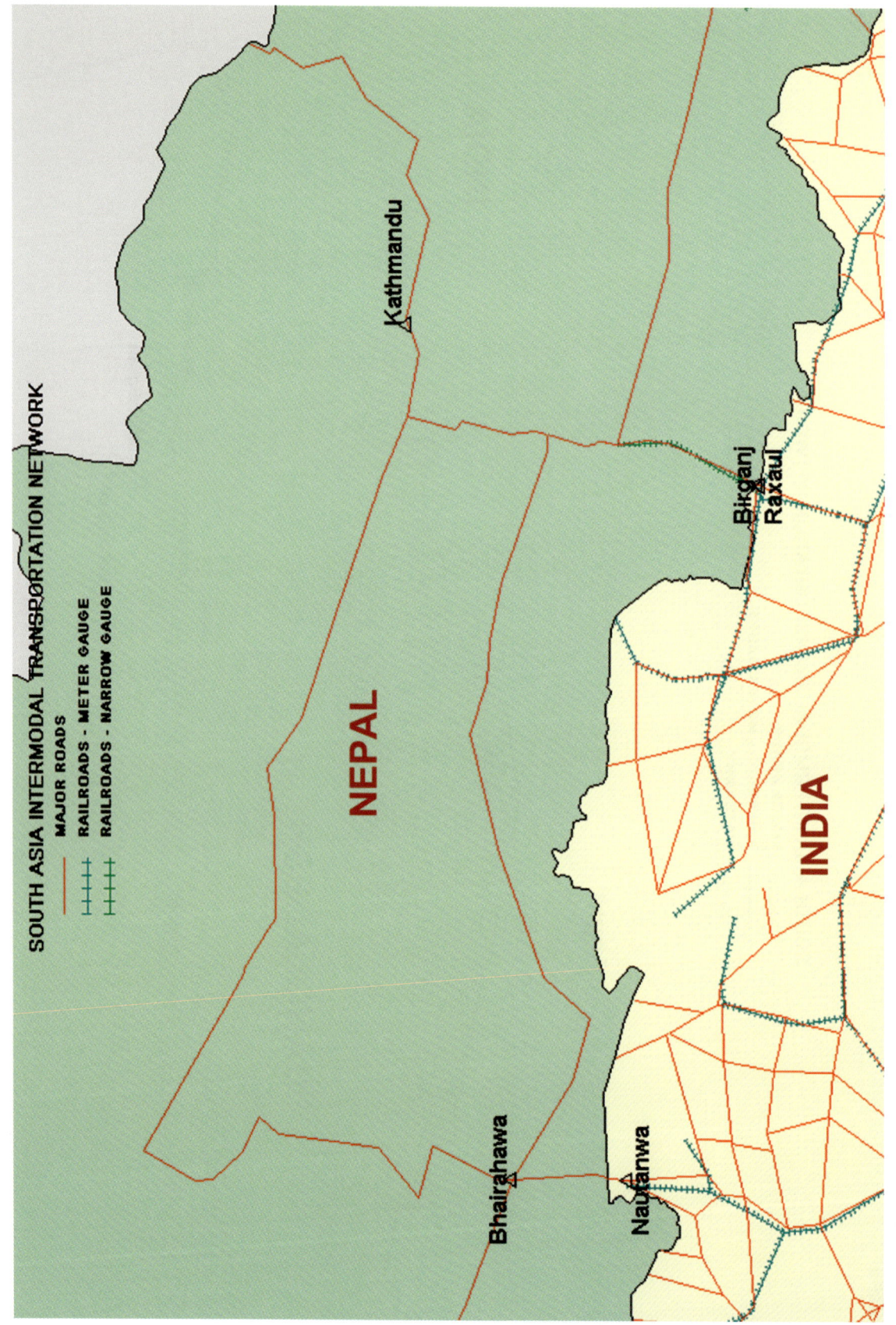

SOUTH ASIA INTERMODAL TRANSPORTATION NETWORK

— MAJOR ROADS
+++ RAILROADS - METER GAUGE
+++ RAILROADS - NARROW GAUGE

NEPAL

INDIA

Kathmandu

Birganj
Raxaul

Bhairahawa

Nautanwa

MAP 5

126

MAP 6

Transport of Carpet from Kathmandu, Nepal to Munich, Germany

| Shipment Size (TEU): | 1 |
| Shipment Value (US$): | $90,000 |

Route A - via Calcutta   **Route B - via Mumbai**

Transport & Handling Costs

		% of Total
Inland Transport	$480	8.385
Cargo Handling	$260	4.542
Ocean Freight	$1,200	20.96

Transport & Handling Time

Inland Transport	117	9.915
Cargo Handling	74	6.271
Ocean Freight	817	69.24

Cross Border Processing Costs

| Cargo Transfer | $258 | 4.507 |
| Customs Inspection | $405 | 7.075 |

Cross Border Processing Time

| Cargo Transfer | 152 | 12.88 |
| Customs Inspection | 20 | 1.695 |

Trade Related Logistics

Time Cost of Goods	$1,637	28.59
Insurance or Pilferage & Damage	$675	11.79
Documentation & Forwarding	$450	7.861
Bank Processing for L/C	$360	6.289

	Cost (US$)	Time (hrs.)
Total:	5725	1180

Transport Logistics Time

Key
Transport and Handling
Cross Border Processing
Trade Related Logistics

TRANSPORT OF CARPET FROM KATHMANDU TO MUNICH, GERMANY
MAJOR ROADS   WATERWAYS
RAILROADS - BROAD GAUGE   ROUTE A: VIA CALCUTTA
RAILROADS - METER GAUGE   ROUTE B: VIA MUMBAI
RAILROADS - NARROW GAUGE

Total Costs

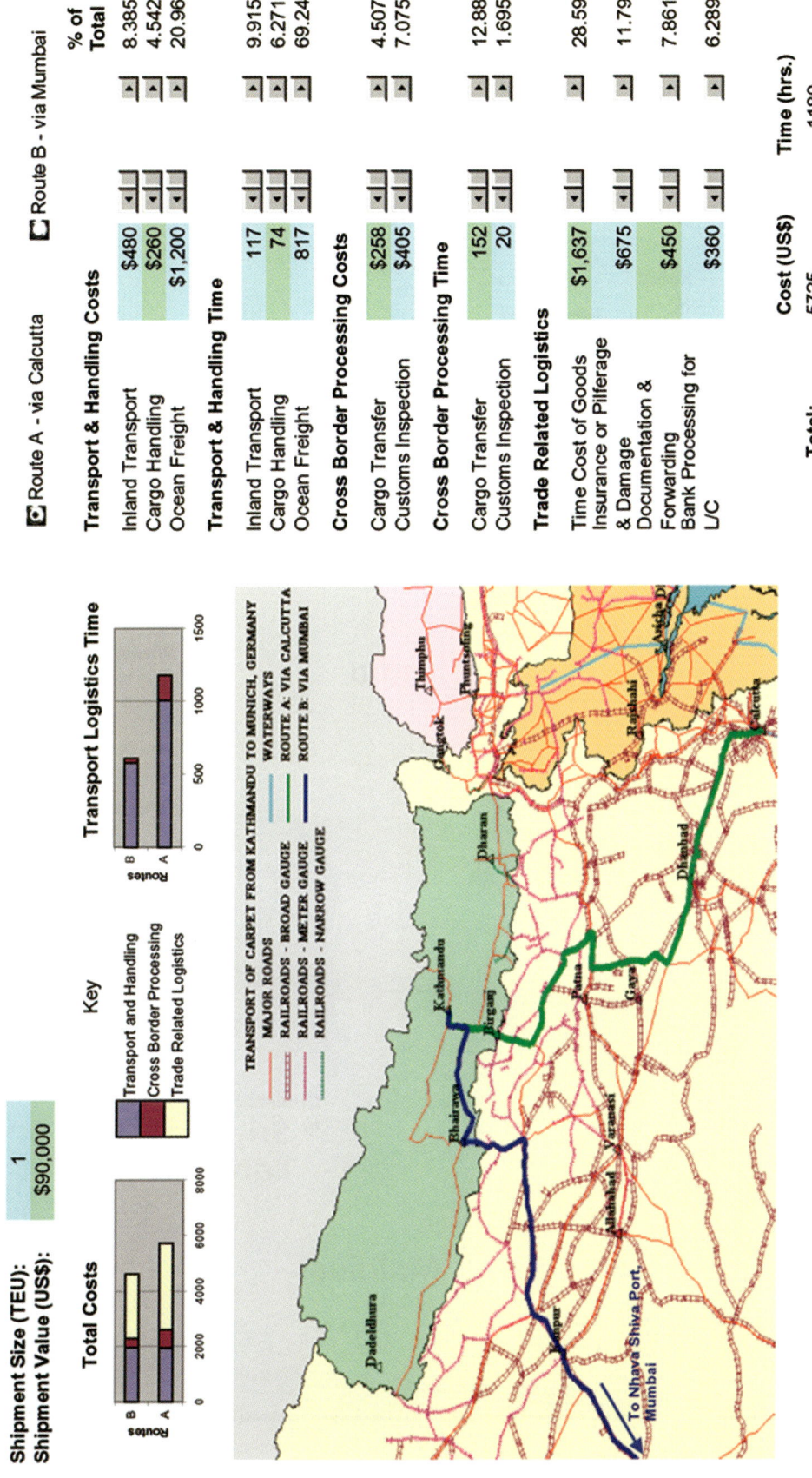

127

MAP 7
IBRD 27291

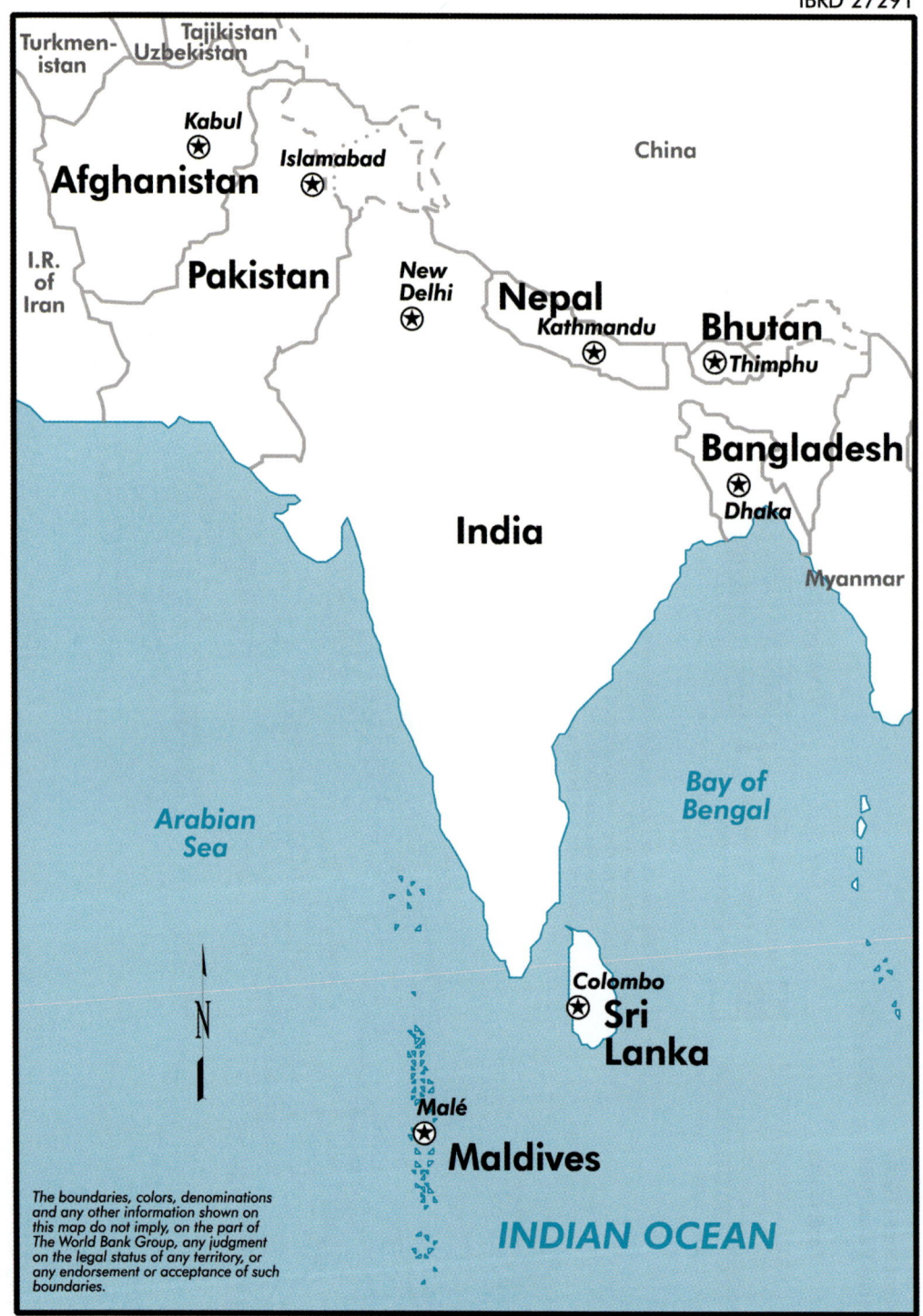

MAP 8

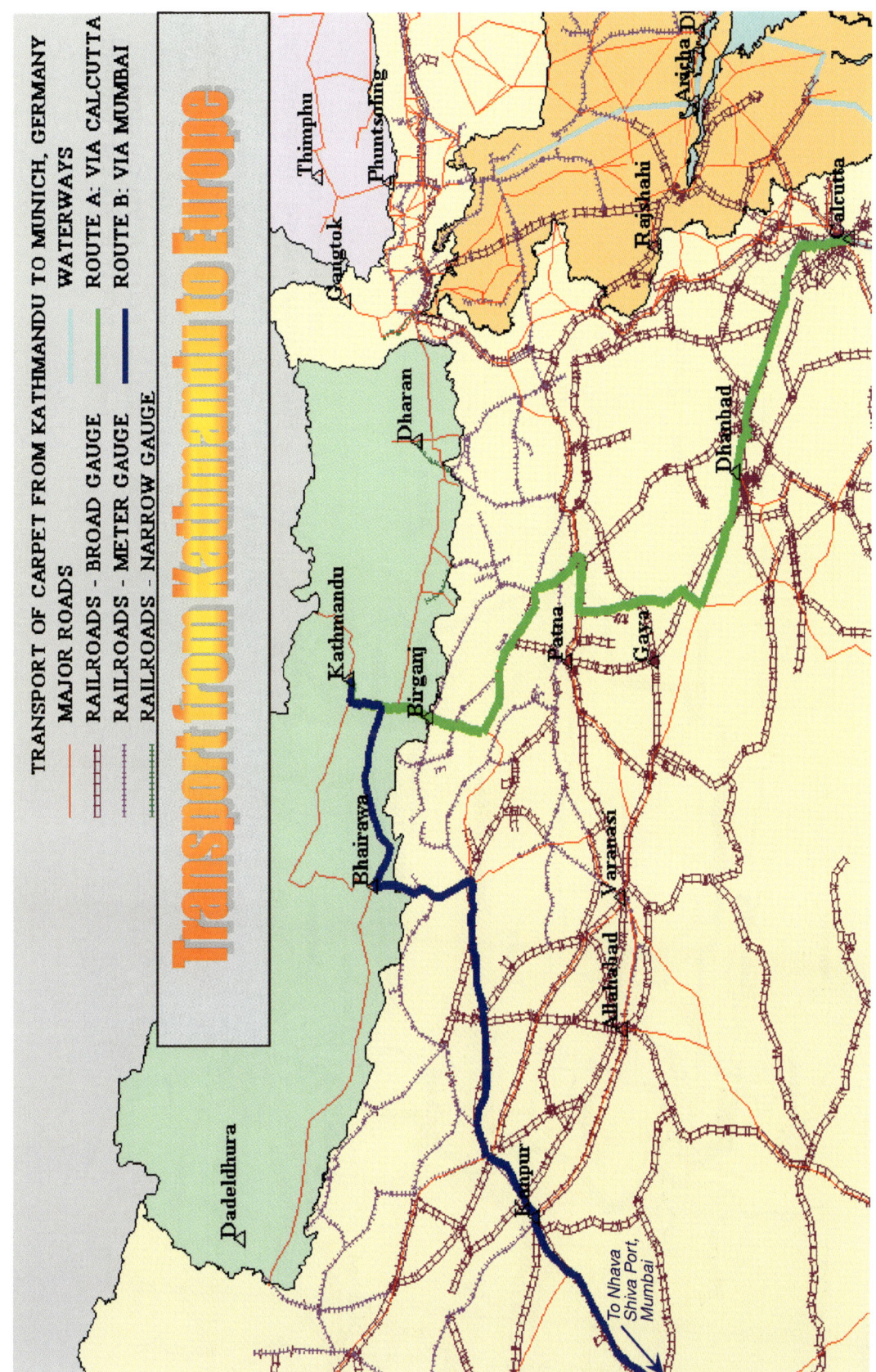

Transport from Kathmandu to Europe

TRANSPORT OF CARPET FROM KATHMANDU TO MUNICH, GERMANY

— MAJOR ROADS

— WATERWAYS

— ROUTE A: VIA CALCUTTA

— ROUTE B: VIA MUMBAI

— RAILROADS - BROAD GAUGE

— RAILROADS - METER GAUGE

— RAILROADS - NARROW GAUGE

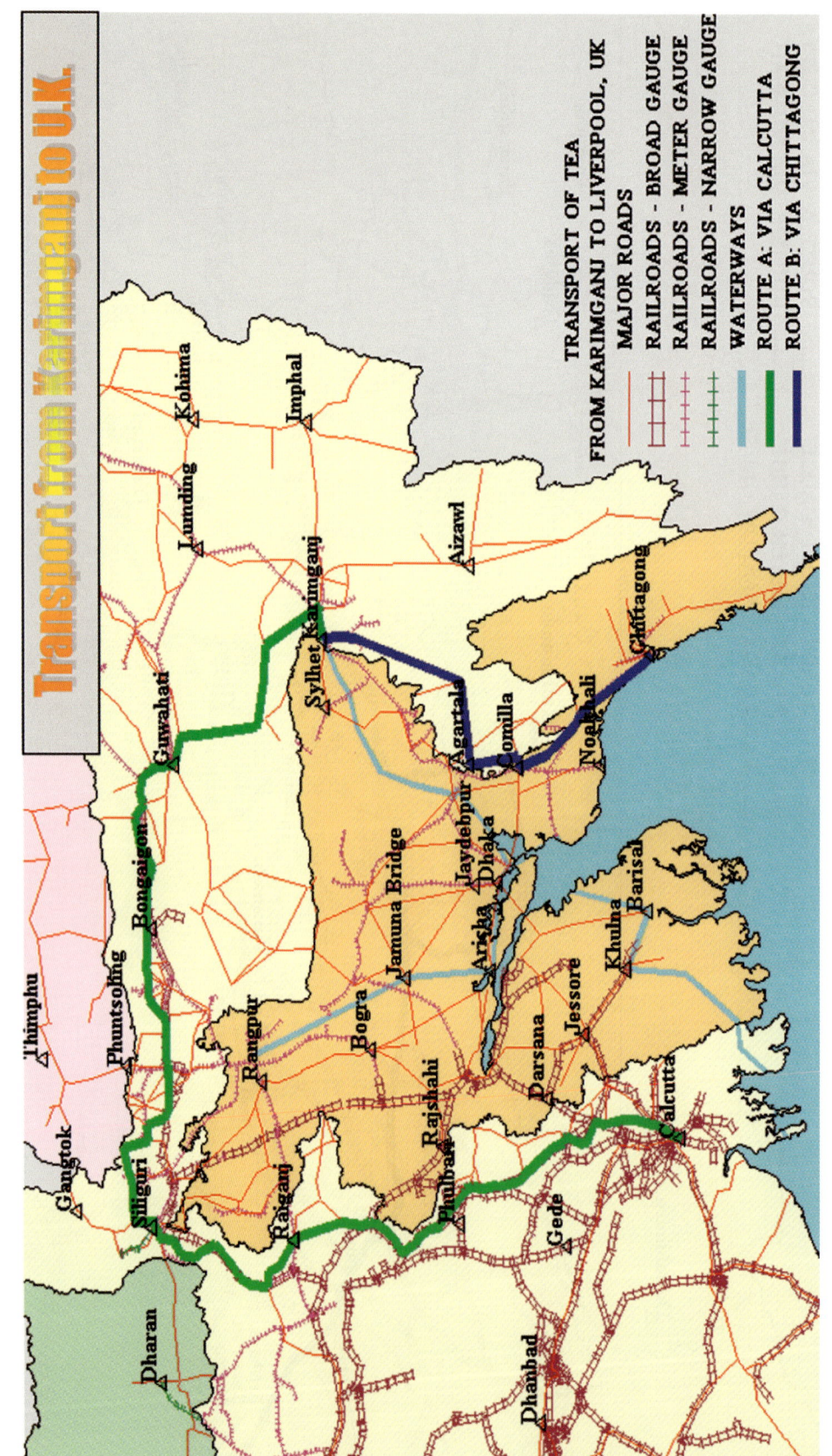

Transport from Karimganj to U.K.

TRANSPORT OF TEA
FROM KARIMGANJ TO LIVERPOOL, UK

MAJOR ROADS
RAILROADS - BROAD GAUGE
RAILROADS - METER GAUGE
RAILROADS - NARROW GAUGE
WATERWAYS
ROUTE A: VIA CALCUTTA
ROUTE B: VIA CHITTAGONG

MAP 9

130

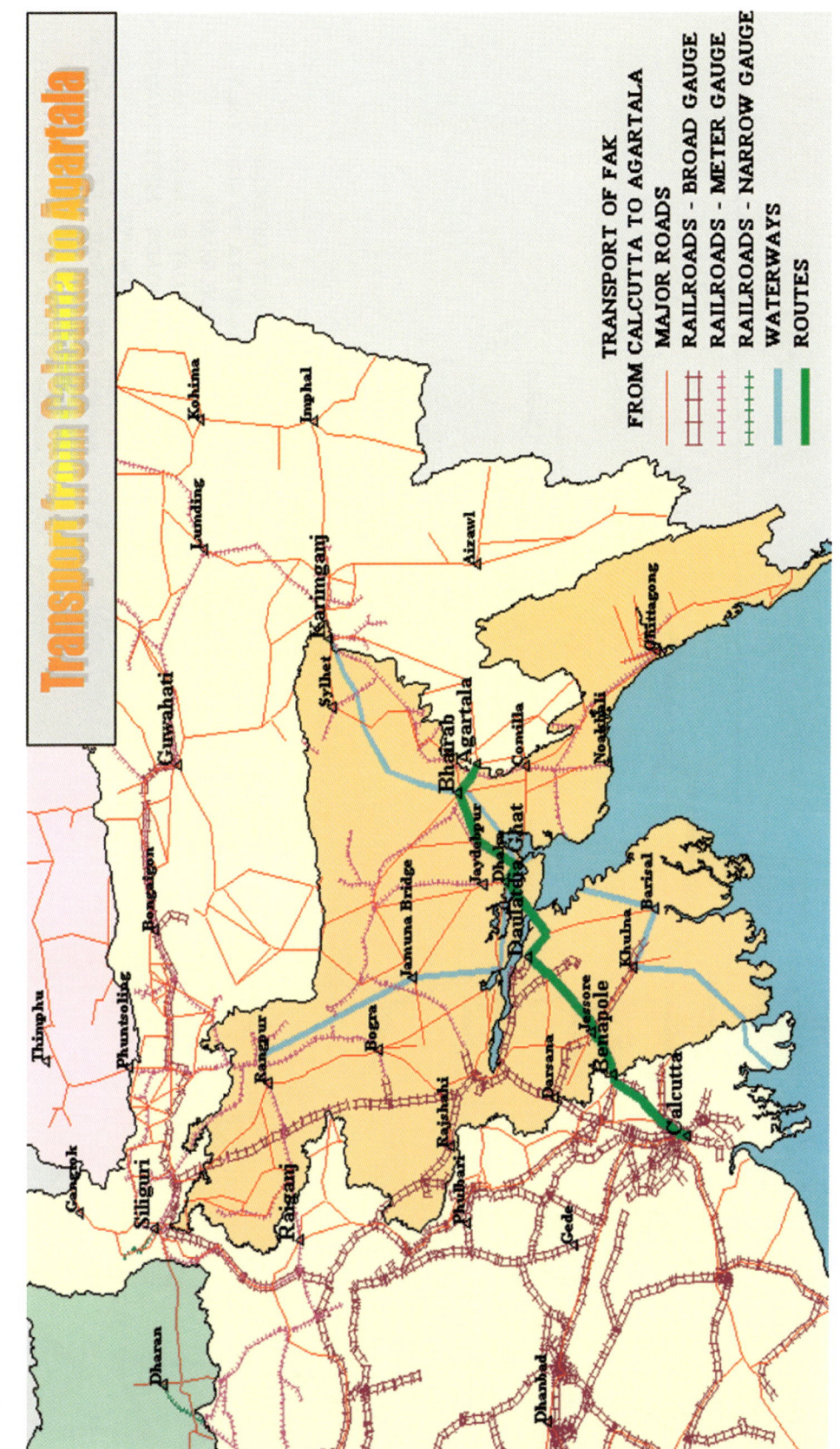

Transport from Calcutta to Agartala

Transport of FAK
From Calcutta to Agartala

- Major Roads
- Railroads - Broad Gauge
- Railroads - Meter Gauge
- Railroads - Narrow Gauge
- Waterways
- Routes

MAP 10

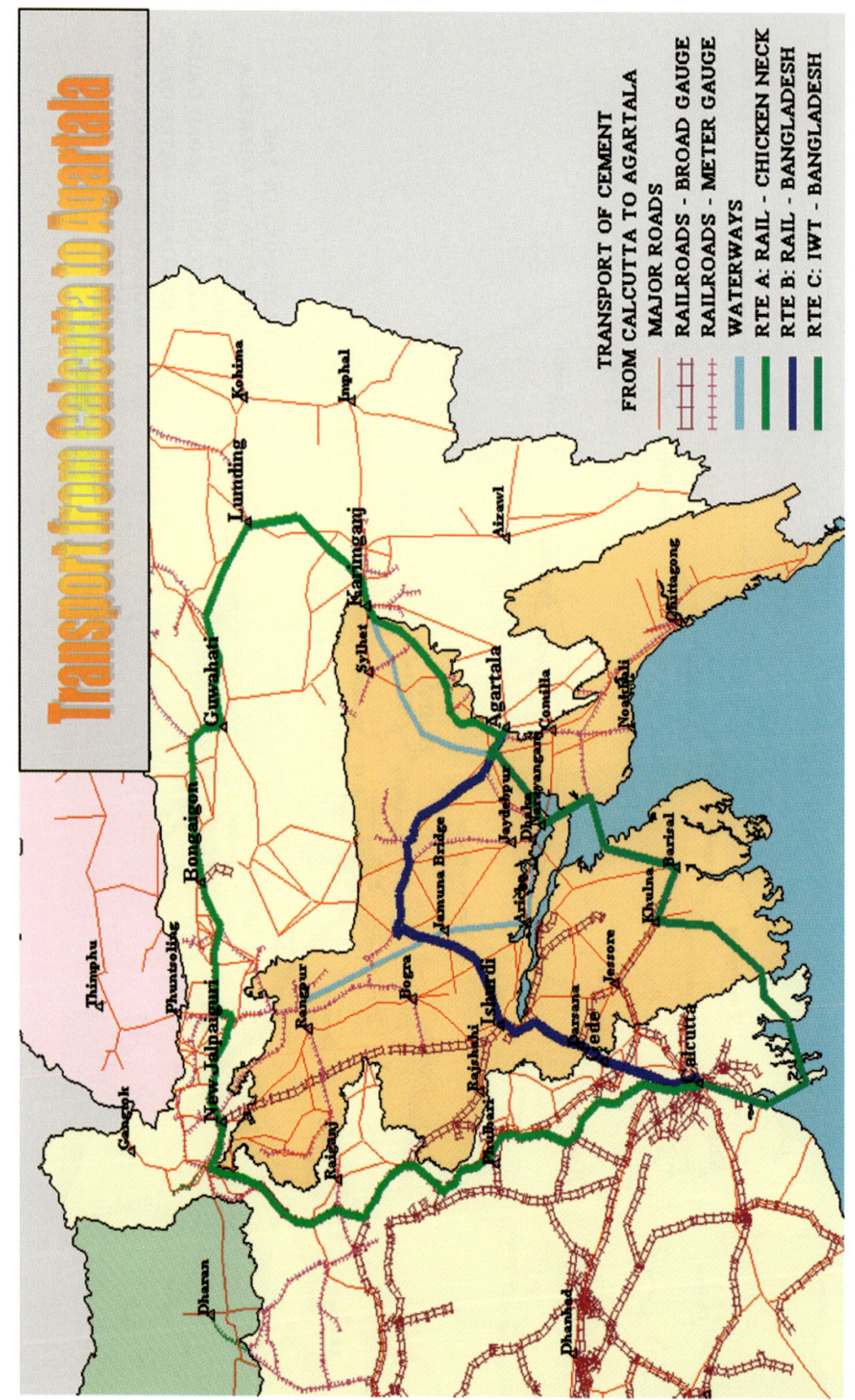

Transport from Calcutta to Agartala

**TRANSPORT OF CEMENT
FROM CALCUTTA TO AGARTALA**

MAJOR ROADS
RAILROADS - BROAD GAUGE
RAILROADS - METER GAUGE
WATERWAYS
RTE A: RAIL - CHICKEN NECK
RTE B: RAIL - BANGLADESH
RTE C: IWT - BANGLADESH

MAP 11

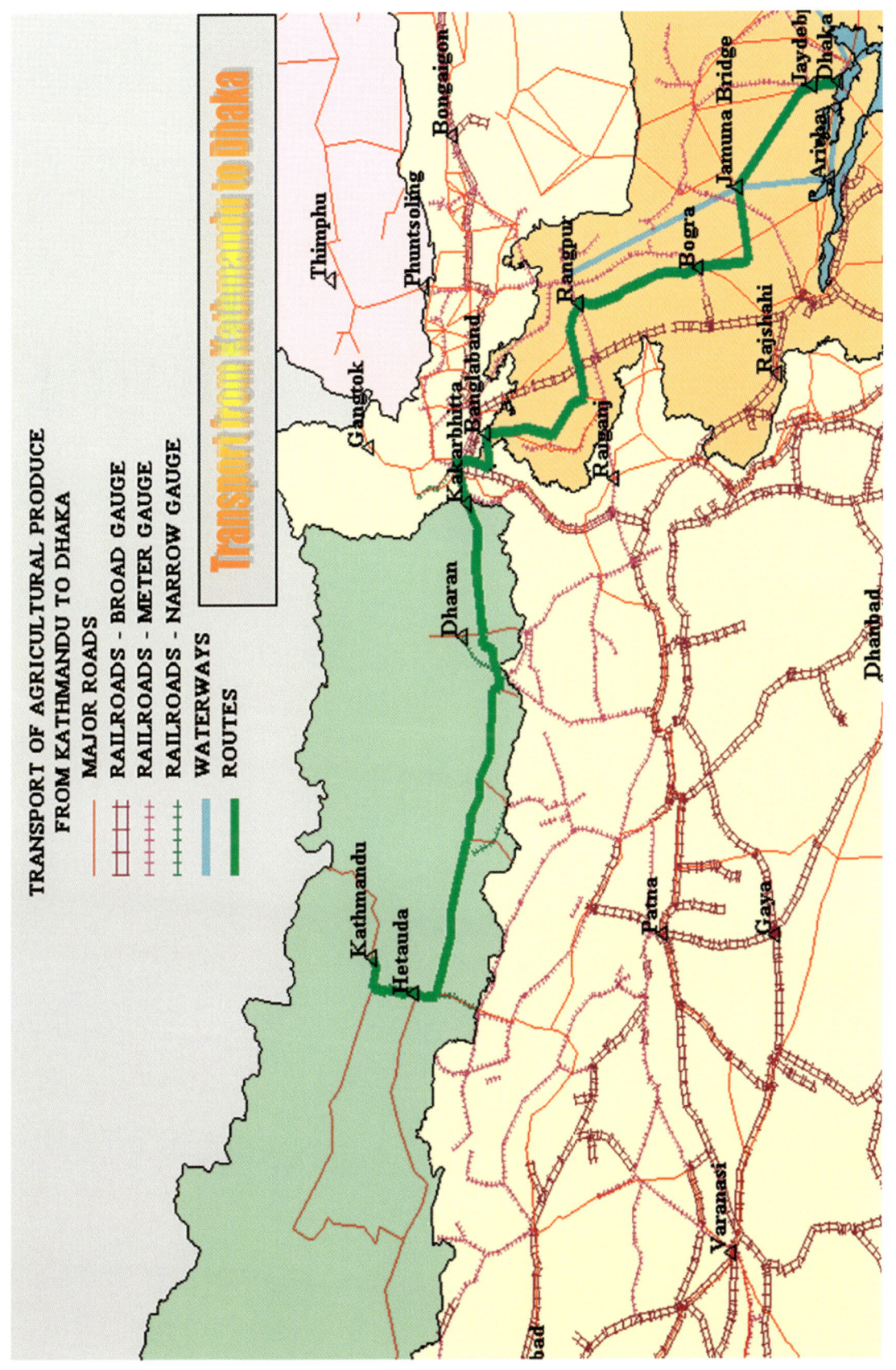

MAP 12

TRANSPORT OF AGRICULTURAL PRODUCE
FROM KATHMANDU TO DHAKA

MAJOR ROADS
RAILROADS - BROAD GAUGE
RAILROADS - METER GAUGE
RAILROADS - NARROW GAUGE
WATERWAYS
ROUTES

Transport from Kathmandu to Dhaka

133